W9-DJN-570

Come With Faith

COME WITH FAITH

Michael Daves

ABINGDON
PRESS

New York
Nashville

COME WITH FAITH

Library of Congress Catalog Card Number: 65-20361

SET UP, PRINTED, AND BOUND BY THE PARTHENON PRESS, AT NASHVILLE TENNESSEE, UNITED STATES OF AMERICA

To Paul Lee

PREFACE

One classic Protestant definition of the church goes: "The visible Church of Christ is a congregation of faithful men in which the pure Word of God is preached, and the Sacraments duly administered according to Christ's ordinance, in all those things that of necessity are requisite to the same."

It has been said that Protestants have adhered only to the first half of the definition, emphasizing the preached Word, while neglecting the sacramental life of the community. Infrequent observance, lack of clear theological understanding, and congregational indifference have often characterized the Protestant attitude toward Holy Communion. Although this judgment is fairly accurate for the past, it is not so for the present. Today, we are witnessing a modern reformation, one in which a sacramental renewal is taking place. Once again, Protestants are recognizing that the bread of life is broken at the table as well as at the pulpit.

The Lord's Supper and Holy Baptism are absolutely essential to a valid proclamation of the Gospel message. Albert C. Outler said, "Any congregation that regularly sings the *Te Deum* in its worship service hears the Gospel whether or not the minister is preaching it." This is even more fundamentally true with the sacraments. They remain most untouched by the whim of the individual minister, calling us back to the central meaning of the gospel message. As Emil Brunner put it: "The Sacraments are the divinely given flying buttresses which save the church from collapse."

Lest anyone think that what I have said downgrades preaching, let me say this: Only in a community where the Word of God is preached can the sacraments be duly administered. Calvin said, "The true ministration of the Sacrament standeth not without the Word." Preaching and sacraments exist as one indivisible whole—two different and necessary ways of communicating the gospel. One cannot be ignored without great harm to the other.

Unless the Sacrament is observed every Sunday, I believe that it is appropriate to substitute a meditation for the sermon on Communion Sunday. The Communion meditation should fulfill certain qualifications: it should help the congregation deepen their understanding of the Eucharist, it should seek to revitalize their faith, and it should be briefer than a sermon. At the same time, it would be improper to note much contrast between the meditation and sermon. Both have the task of proclaiming the Word of God to contemporary man so that he will respond in obedience and trust.

Most of these meditations were first delivered at First Methodist Church of Holliday, Texas. For the encouragement, loyalty, and faith of this congregation I shall be forever grateful.

I am in special debt to Mrs. Carlton Carr for typing the manuscript and to Mrs. Marvin Moody for many helpful suggestions. My wife, Patty, also deserves much credit. She has seen me through several books now, and remains my best critic.

Michael Daves

CONTENTS

Seasonal Meditations

General Meditations

Seasonal Meditations

Advent
WAITING FOR GOD

In Samuel Beckett's play *Waiting for Godot* nothing happens because no one knows how to make anything happen. The main characters, Estragon and Vladimir, would kill themselves if they knew how to go about it. At another time, they would celebrate their friendship, but they have forgotten how to celebrate. Once, Vladimir asks: "Well, what do we do?" Estragon replies: "Don't let's do anything. It's safer." Then this exchange takes place:

> *Vladimir:* Let's wait and see what he says.
> *Estragon:* Who?
> *Vladimir:* Godot.
> *Estragon:* Good idea.
> *Vladimir:* Let's wait until we know exactly how we stand.
> *Estragon:* On the one hand it might be better to strike the iron before it freezes.

Vladimir: I'm curious to hear what he has to offer. Then we'll take it or leave it.[1]

Waiting for Godot. It's intolerable, a terrible strain on the nerves. "Nothing happens, nobody comes, nobody goes, it's awful." Estragon and Vladimir decide to leave at the end of both acts. "Well, shall we?" "Yes, let's go." But the stage directions are: *They do not move.* Godot himself never appears in the play, but a messenger boy comes. The message is brief: "Mr. Godot told me to tell you he won't come this evening but surely tomorrow." Toward the end of the play, the boy appears again. Vladimir knows that the message will be the same: not today, but tomorrow. He asks, "What does he do, Mr. Godot?" (Silence.) "Do you hear me?" Boy: "Yes, Sir." Vladimir: "Well?" Boy: "He does nothing, Sir." Realizing that Godot did not come again, Estragon asks: "And if we dropped him? (Pause.) If we dropped him?" Vladimir answers simply: "He'd punish us." They talk again of suicide, but have no rope and Estragon's belt is too short. Finally Vladimir says: "We'll hang ourselves tomorrow. (Pause.) Unless Godot comes." Estragon asks: "And if he comes?" Vladimir: "We'll be saved." The curtain falls, and they still wait.

Samuel Beckett's play is a commentary on the religious situation. Men wait for God. Godot is Beckett's symbol for God. We wait and carry on meaningless conversation. A spark of hope that God will come soon is quickly extinguished by the dark night. Sometimes, we reach the end of our rope and threaten to hang ourselves tomorrow unless God comes. If he comes, we will be saved. But we have really lost faith in God's coming. It is as if we were orphans in God's universe—lonely, anxious children without a Father to call to. We yearn to say God, but we can only honestly say man. We long to pray, but end up by talking to ourselves. Our situation is like a man walking home through a dark neighborhood. The lights of his bus have disappeared in the darkness; the street lights and house lights are turned out. The street is full of dangers; there are spectors lurking behind every bush. The slightest sound is a source of fear. His pace quickens. He is running headlong into the darkness. How he wishes that someone were with him, someone to hold his hand and to whisper, "Peace, be still!" But modern man thinks he knows that this is not possible, and so he runs, a victim of terrible anxiety.

"God is dead!" cried Nietzsche and gave voice to the feelings of his generation. He portrays a madman searching for God, calling out for him, and finally concluding that he and all men have killed him. The man's hearers do not understand his words, and he believes that he has come with his message too early. He enters the churches and sings his *requiem alternam deo:* "What are these churches now if they are not the tombs and sepulchers of God?" Arthur Koestler perhaps speaks for our generation: "God is dethroned; and although the incognisant masses are tardy in realising the event, they feel the icy draught caused by that vacancy. Man enters upon a spiritual ice age; the established churches can no longer provide more than Eskimo huts where their shivering flock huddles together." [2] Isn't the description of ours as a "post-Christian" era accurate? And is there really anything we can do about it?

God has been used as a stopgap for man's ignorance. As religious people, we often speak of God only when our human perception is at an end; God is called in either as a way of solving insoluble problems or as an aid and comfort in life's extreme situations. But this kind of God is truly dead. Man's science has replaced him, and we should be grateful for man's newfound maturity, his "coming of age." Christians should be able to say, "This God—the God of our illusions—is dead. Thanks be to the real God."

This is the central paradox of the Christian faith: God comes in his not coming, he is glorified in his humiliation, he is present in his absence, he is victorious in his defeat, he lives in his death. God allows himself to be nothing to man, for this is precisely the only way he can become everything. God is Sovereign, but man is free. And when God comes, he does not come coercing the freedom of man. He comes in love and meekness—as an infant lowly—wooing man to repentance. As Dietrich Bonhoeffer put it: "God is teaching us that we must live as men who can get along very well without him. . . . Before God and with him we live without God. God allows himself to be edged out of the world and on-to the cross. God is weak and powerless in the world, and that is exactly the way, the only way, in which he can be with us and help us." [3]

Isn't this truth vividly portrayed in the Christmas story? Jesus Christ, the Savior of men, came quietly and unobtrusively through the world's back door.

How silently, how silently
The wondrous gift is given!

He was born not a conquering Roman, but a defeated Jew; born not in a great city, but in a town which today has less than two thousand homes—Bethlehem. From the very first, the world was inhospitable to him. His birth came in a stable because there was no "room in the inn." He grew into manhood, but he was unwilling to exercise his powers to spellbind and to cower the crowds into the kingdom of God. By all our earthly standards, he was a complete and miserable failure. We call him King, and King he is. But a strange and ironic King. His only crown was a crown of thorns and his only throne was a cross on which he died. The scandal of Christianity—yet at the same time its very essence—is the powerless power of Christ as he empties out himself for us men and our salvation.

Vladimir and Estragon did not know the Christmas story; they did not know the Christian story. They waited for Godot—the traditional God who doesn't exist. Godot had a white beard; he punished those who rejected him; he never came; he was always off stage. The only reason Vladimir and Estragon didn't drop him was that they were afraid of punishment.

Still there is something of the Christian story in *Waiting for Godot.* The landscape is completely dead except for a tree. Could the tree symbolize the tree on which Christ died? Vladimir and Estragon wait by the tree, but they are unaware of its having any meaning. Christians themselves can be unaware of its meaning. On the cross, the whole life of Jesus is offered up as "a full, perfect and sufficient sacrifice" to God. The power of God is shown in the weakness of the cross; the acceptance of God is revealed in the abandonment of Jesus. "My God, my God, why hast thou forsaken me?"

Advent is a season of waiting and preparation for the Nativity of Jesus the Christ. At Christmas, the word of the church will be that God has decisively revealed himself in Jesus Christ. But in Advent, we need to hear another word: we exist as people waiting. We are people "between the times," who live between the Lord's first coming and his second coming. So we must wait. But we do not wait without hope—our hope is in the name of the Lord who made heaven and earth. Our world has been radically affected by the Christ Event. "The light shines in the darkness, and the darkness has not overcome it." We wait, but not hopeless, discouraged, suicidal persons, like Vladimir and Estragon waiting for their Godot. Our God may be dead; still we have faith that there is a God beyond the death of our God. God is hidden even in his revelation in Jesus Christ and we see him through a dark glass; still we believe that one day he will appear in glory. Until then, we must understand that the silence of God is his speaking, the abandonment of God is his acceptance, and his crucifixion at the hands of sinful man is a prelude to the overture of resurrection.

We participate in the Lord's Supper, and what a sacrament of hopeful waiting it is! For, as Paul said, whenever we take this meal we "proclaim the Lord's death until he comes." We take the bread and wine into our bodies —the symbols of his suffering and dereliction—and so identify ourselves with him in his sacrifice. We are bidden to come and die. But the Lord's Supper is not to be observed with downcast hearts. It is a joyful event, for the Lord's death points to his resurrection and coming again. We are bidden to come and live.

We wait, not with our eyes closed, for we are called to be watchmen. "Watch therefore, for you do not know on what day your Lord is coming" (Matt. 24:42). In the Old Testament, the usual responsibility of watchmen on the city wall was to sound the alarm when the enemy approached. The prophets, however, understood that their responsibility as watchmen was to discern the approach of the Lord in the events of history and to announce this to the people. The call to watch means to discern the signs of the times, to know what hour it is, to be ready for the Lord's coming. When he comes to the door of our hearts, do we recognize that it is he? Time and again, he has left, unnoticed. For he comes in his weakness and not coming. He comes in the headline of the daily newspaper that challenges us to take a moral stand. He comes in the terrified eyes of a Negro being chased by police dogs. He comes in the hunger and loneliness of men the world over. It is not obvious that he comes. He is hidden in the neighbor's need and in the events of history. So, we must pray for "eyes to see and ears to hear" his coming. We cannot wait passively like Vladimir and Estragon, carrying on a meaningless conversation. We must wait actively, carrying on a meaningful service. We must want the Lord to come more than we want anything else. He must be our total diet.

> I wait for the Lord, my soul waits,
> and in his word I hope;
> my soul waits for the Lord
> more than watchmen for the
> morning,
> more than watchmen for the
> morning (Ps. 130:5-6).

Christmastide

GOD'S GREAT TRIP

John 1:14

In his delightful book *Travels with Charley,* John Steinbeck told of his neighbors' reaction when they learned he was to take a leisurely three-month tour of America in a custom-made camper: "I saw in their eyes something I was to see over and over in every part of the nation—a burning desire to go, to move, to get under way, anyplace, away from any Here. . . . Nearly every American hungers to move." [1]

Yes, Americans have a perpetual romance with roaming. Even the ones who say, "I don't like to travel," love to read about it! The sum and substance of our nation's history is this: a people on the move, never satisfied with what they found, pushing back frontiers, fording rivers, chopping away forests, digging for treasure, climbing mountains, driving cattle, inventing better means of transportation, and laying roads to travel on. "Go west, young man, go west" is our real national anthem.

Perhaps our deep desire to travel is one reason the Christmas story appeals to us so—for that's what it's all about—traveling. Joseph and Mary were traveling from Nazareth to Bethlehem. Not a very long way, you say? Only about sixty miles? According to modern standards, that's a very short trip; many commute farther to work every day. But when transportation was by beast or on foot, sixty miles was a tiring journey. They were traveling to Bethlehem—not for pleasure or for profit—but simply to fulfill the requirements of a new Roman law that each person be enrolled in his native city. It was there in Bethlehem's lowly stable that Jesus was born. Soon after his birth, the Holy Family took another trip—this one longer and harder. Threatened by the rage of Herod, they fled into the safety of Egypt where their people had been called from bondage centuries earlier. Finally, when they learned of Herod's death, they returned to the village of Nazareth where Jesus grew "in wisdom and in stature, and in favor with God and man." There are three trips recorded in the Gospels: the trip from Nazareth to Bethlehem, from Bethlehem to Egypt, and from Egypt back again to Nazareth.

And there is also a fourth trip—one not made by the Holy Family, but the most vital, perhaps the longest, certainly the costliest trip of all. It is the trip made by God himself. "And the Word became flesh and dwelt among us, full of grace and truth; we have beheld his glory, glory as of the only Son from the Father." In Jesus Christ, God made a great trip and became one with human kind. He felt the cold winds of the world in his face, he was stabbed by rejection, torn by temptation, and, finally, hung on a cross to die. Perhaps a parable will help make clearer the meaning of God's incarnation:

Once upon a time, there lived a King who had power over all the nations and all peoples. His courts were of richest splendor; his tables were heavy with finest food. Music and laughter and gaiety floated from inside the castle and it was always light. Clouds wrapped the castle in an ethereal majesty. Travelers always stopped and looked at the castle for a long while, wishing they might know the King who built the marvelous structure. But none were able to reach the castle.

In the cold of winter, the King's tailor entered the royal chambers with his latest sketches for the King's wardrobe. The little man was proud of his accomplishments. He had selected the finest materials and weaved them into the most beautiful garments that eyes had ever beheld. They glittered like gold.

But the King was not pleased. He ordered his tailor out, vowing to make his own clothes. No one but the King himself knew what he wanted. The door to the throne room was shut and locked. Weeks passed, and from inside came the clack-clack-clacking of the loom. The royal court waited with great anticipation to see what the King would make for himself. They knew they were bound to be blinded by the glory of it. Finally, the awaited day arrived. The doors opened and the King appeared.

Everyone—especially the tailor—gasped in surprise and horror. His Majesty was dressed in the simplest, cheapest, most unkingly garments imaginable. He had the choice of the finest materials in the world, but he chose to wear—the clothes of a beggar!

"I am going into the valley," he said quietly.[2]

It is a long, long trip from lofty heights to lowly valley—from castle to cross—from power to powerlessness. The God who was the Creator of heaven and earth became the Redeemer of men in Jesus Christ. He emptied himself out for man, became as one of us.

Christianity is the religion of the Incarnation. The truth is so simple that it is often forgotten: There would be no Christianity without the Incarnation. For us, this event is the turning point in history. Our lives, as well as our calendars, are dated B.C. and A.D. The difference between Christianity and religions of no incarnation is the difference between reading a play and watching it performed. I read Eugene O'Neill's *Long Day's Journey into Night* before I ever saw it on the stage. It was exciting to read—yet something was missing. That "something" was added when I saw it performed. The lines came from actors. The play had movement and depth. It had become alive. The words were incarnated in persons. Or, to put it another way: The difference between Christianity and religions of no incarnation is the difference between receiving a letter from a loved one and having the loved one embrace you. A letter is cold compared to the actual presence of the one you love.

God did not send us a manuscript of a play or a letter. Rather, he acted out the drama of our salvation. He embraced us in Jesus Christ. God did not play it safe in a warm castle, but risked the streets of the village. He did not hide behind the clouds, but revealed his love on a cross.

But wait! We cannot speak of Incarnation without Resurrection and Ascension. For Jesus Christ, who perfectly expressed the Father's love and purpose, was raised from the dead, "ascended into heaven, and sitteth at the right hand of God the Father Almighty." What do these strange words from the creed mean? Martin Luther made them clear when he said "the right hand of God is everywhere." In other words, the Incarnation which had its occurrence in the "fullness of time" cannot be limited in its benefits. Jesus Christ is at the right hand of God—he is everywhere! God's Incarnation is not only to the inhabitants of ancient Bethlehem two thousand years ago; his Incarnation is a present reality for all who have faith. So we can sing today:

> O holy Child of Bethlehem!
> Descend to us, we pray;
> Cast out our sin, and enter in,
> Be born in us today.

The Word becomes flesh in our lives, too. God makes his trip into our common ways as well. I remember a simple woodcut that caught this truth. At the top of the woodcut was the star of Bethlehem, its light shining into the city below. But the city was not Bethlehem; it was a modern city with tall buildings and factories. In the foreground a road led to the city, and people were traveling toward the star. *Not* the shepherds, *not* the wise men, but a soldier, a priest, a factory worker, a housewife—men and women in modern dress.

If Christianity is the religion of the Incarnation, its sacraments are sacraments of Incarnation. Holy Communion reminds us of historical events that took place long ago, and for this we are thankful. In this way, the sacrament can be regarded as a memorial. But it is infinitely more. The Lord's Supper is not only about the past; it is a holy highway for God's approach to man in the present. In this sacrament, God comes, seals his love to us, and quickens our faith. We discover that ours is the fullness of time, that our town is Bethlehem, and that God makes his long, lonely journey into our lives. As we kneel here at the Lord's Table, the Word becomes flesh and dwells among us, full of grace and truth; we behold his glory.

New Year's

GOD AND OUR ANXIETY

Matt. 6:25 John 16:33

Anxiety, like sin, is a dogged fact of life. We might wish it away, but it stubbornly stays—like an unwanted dinner guest. W. H. Auden has called our times the "age of anxiety," an epithet that could be applied to almost any period in human history. Man has always been plagued by anxiety, if we are to believe ancient literature and art.

Think of how anxiety hung over the Middle Ages like a pall over a coffin. Society was glued together by magic, mystery, and miracle. Poor peasants hid behind closed doors, fearful that the Horseman Death would whisk them away. The best sellers of the time were not how to escape paying income tax, but how to escape hell. Such works as *On the Art of Dying* portrayed in lurid woodcuts the departing spirit encircled by fiends enticing him to commit the unpardonable sin of abandoning God's mercy. In 1493, a woodcut displayed the Judgment Day. Christ the Judge sits on a rainbow. A lily, signifying the redeemed, protrudes from his right ear; from his left ear, a sword, symbolizing the doom of the damned. Below, the angels are ushering the saved into paradise, while the devils drag the damned from their tombs and throw them into the flames of hell. To escape the judgment to come, men laid hold of the help which the church had to offer, especially the sacraments. And it would not be unlikely that a man could enter the monastery to save his own soul. Such was the case with a young man named Martin Luther.[1]

Every age could be called the "age of anxiety," but we are more concerned with our age than those long dead. Our anxiety is more important to us than that of Martin Luther simply because we must somehow deal with it.

Whether we admit it or not, we are anxiety-ridden. I remember talking to a high school student about T. S. Eliot's poem, *The Hollow Men.* "Hollow?" he said, "I don't dig it! What does he mean by hollow men?" I explained that for Eliot, "hollow" was symbolic of modern man's emptiness and estrangement. He still didn't "dig it." He replied, "That's crazy. Everybody I know is happy and content." Obviously, he didn't know his friends in depth—including himself. For you can often scratch a happy person and find a miserable wretch. Remember the story of the Glasgow physician who examined a patient in deep despair. He said, "There is nothing wrong with you. Go hear Grumaldi, the clown, and laugh and you will be well." The patient answered, "I am Grumaldi."

If we are such hearty, healthy, happy people, why do nearly twenty thousand of us commit suicide in the United States every year? Why are there four million alcoholics? And why are half a million Americans patients in mental hospitals? Contented Americans swallow nineteen thousand sleeping pills a night—seven million a year. That represents over $60,000,000 a year spent! We gulp down eleven million pounds of aspirin each year—seventeen billion aspirin tablets. A *New Yorker* cartoon shows a harassed executive gazing out of the window and murmuring, "Ah, for the good old days when we had nothing to fear except fear itself."

To understand anxiety, we must examine its linguistic root. It comes from the Latin *angustiae,* which means constriction of breathing. Anxiety is a feeling of "shut-upness," as Kierkegaard would say, or of "No Exit," as Sartre would put it. Unlike fear, anxiety has no definite object. In this respect, fear is always preferable to anxiety. For at least the enemy is out in the open where he can be fought. "I am afraid of not having enough money to pay my bills." "I am afraid of failing in my vocation." "I am afraid of busting out of school." These are fears which have an object and are more easily analyzed and fought. The cause of anxiety, however, is indefinite. Anxiety is never out in the open, but attacks us from ambush. Anxiety is like a knife in the back instead of a gun at the stomach. It is the devil's sneak attack.

But we go astray if we consider anxiety only in individualistic terms. It is not merely my individual breathing which is constricted by this strange force. It is the breathing of the whole world—the very structures of reality. Anxiety not only is a threat to our individual being, but also threatens to shake the foundations. The whole world is called into question. All that we have counted valuable and hoped in is swept away by the flood of anxiety, and we live in a wasteland where there is no God, no hope, no life, no light. (This is much more awesome, you see, than personal fear. For, if I fear that I cannot make ends meet, I always have the hope that I will be able to get extra employment. If I am fearful of failing in my vocation, I always have the hope that I will somehow pull out of the slump. If I am fearful of busting out of school, there is always the possibility that the professors will show mercy.) But this cosmic anxiety allows me no hope, for the very structures of reality are torn asunder and I am left with an absurd nothingness. In this twilight of the gods, men roam through the streets like the blind Oedipus with no chance of seeing again.

Anxiety as a threat to our being becomes even more acute on the threshold of a new year. There is something radically different about approaching a calendar and tearing away the month of November than the month of December. For when we come to this month—there is nothing left on the calendar! It is the end of the year, the beginning of another one. This phenomenon makes us realize that we do not control the passing of the seasons—years come and go, life comes and goes, completely beyond our control. As a sentence of "O God Our Help in Ages Past"—squeamishly eliminated from some hymnals—goes:

> Time, like an ever-rolling stream,
> Bears all its sons away. . . .

Our acute anxiety as we face a new year goes a long way toward explaining the forced levity that accompanies the new year's celebration. Some people are not so much welcoming in a new year—"ring out the old, ring in the new"—as they are trying to bury their anxieties in liquor, confetti, and assorted forms of gaiety.

> Faces along the bar
> Cling to their average day:
> The lights must never go out
> The music must always play. . . .
> Lest we should see where we are,
> Lost in a haunted wood,
> Children afraid of the night
> Who have never been happy or good.[2]

But what of Christianity? Is Christianity simply another escape from anxiety—a spiritual martini? Is it only a matter of choosing which escape you want and then taking it? If this is true, then most would choose the Epicurean philosophy of "eat, drink, and be merry, for tomorrow you die" above the gloom and glum displayed by many Christians. And who could blame them?

The criticism that Christianity is an escape from anxiety should be faced squarely. Freud, you recall, examined professedly religious patients, found they were trying to escape from life, and proceeded to write God off as "the projection of the human father figure." Very neat—too neat in fact! Because some Christians often show indications of exchanging their freedom for an authoritarian safety, it does not follow that the essence of Christianity is escapism. This only proves how far Christians have strayed from the mind of Christ.

Christianity at its best faces anxiety. At this point, Christians and pagans are no different: they both are plagued by anxiety. And the Christian, who believes in the providence of God, may have a tougher time coming to terms with anxiety than the pagan who expects nothing from God. Yet from his wrestling with reality, the Christian finds that at the bottom of life God, and not anxiety, has the final word. Christianity is no escape from anxiety, but a genuine way of conquering it.

When we soliloquize "to be or not to be" and are burdened down by the "slings and arrows of outrageous fortune," we turn to the One who overcame anxiety, the One in whom the new being was manifest. Jesus

Christ looked at the lilies of the field and the birds of the air and exclaimed, "Do not be anxious about tomorrow." On the eve of his crucifixion, he confided to his disciples, "In this world you have tribulation; but be of good cheer, I have overcome the world." There you have the realism of Jesus briefly put—and the realism of the whole New Testament. Paul spoke of nothing separating us from the love of God in Jesus Christ our Lord, but this was no escape. He had come to terms with every possible event that would separate us from God's love—and found them powerless before the power of God's love.

Jesus Christ does not erase our anxieties; he helps us live creatively with our anxiety. The Christian man—like any other man—knows meaninglessness. He feels guilt. And the Christian man knows that some day he, too, must die. Still we are not left comfortless. God deals with our anxiety by giving us the courage to exist in spite of the negative forces of life. God deals with our anxieties by joining himself to us in Jesus Christ and taking our fears, hurts, and disappointments into himself.

We can lay our anxieties before him and in him find a power of being greater than ourselves, our world, and the evil powers. We have our anxieties, but they have changed: they are no longer an ultimate threat to our being. Our "shut-upness" is not ours to face alone—it has become God's "shut-upness" too. W. E. Sangster knew this to be true. When he lay dying as an invalid, he wrote from his bed: "I am shut up with God, and that is a wonderful thing."

A little boy could not go to sleep in his dark room. His imagination played tricks on him: monsters, waiting to devour him, were lurking in the darkness. So, naturally he cried and cried until his father came. Sensing what was wrong, his father promised him, "I'll leave your door open a crack." So, with the light and warmth of another room—the room where his parents were—flowing into his, the little boy fell to sleep. It was still dark, but there was light enough for the little boy to see that his monsters were only furniture.

When I am in the Father's house, I can rest secure even in the darkness, for by the light which shines in Jesus Christ I am shown that my monsters are only furniture. I am persuaded that nothing can wrest me from his love and care, whether I am awake or asleep, whether I live or die. The Sacrament of the Lord's Supper represents this security for us as we face the new year.

Epiphany

THE LIGHT OF THE WORLD

John 8:12

Now when Jesus was born in Bethlehem of Judea in the days of Herod the King, behold, there came wise men from the university to Jerusalem.

Saying, Where is the bright new star we have followed so far? We have traveled many miles over desert and mountains to get a closer look. Herod assembled the chief priests and scribes of the people and demanded of them where the star could best be seen.

And they said unto him, In Bethlehem of Judea, for thus it is written in the astrology maps.

The wise men started on the dusty road to Bethlehem, their camels laden down with microscopes and telescopes and gyroscopes. And slide rules.

And when they saw the star, they rejoiced with exceeding great joy. The learned professors of the university, followed faithfully by their adoring students, looked for the best place to view the new constellation. After a long search, they finally set up their instruments outside a stable and made notes as to the shape and size of the star. Amazing! Fantastic! Like no other star! they exclaimed.

Noise from the stable disrupted their calculations and exclamations. One of the students approached the stable, opened the door, and said,

Madame, please keep that Baby from crying. We are trying to record a great new astronomical discovery, and the noise is distracting.[1]

Wise men from the university are not alone in missing the central meaning of the great Christmas and Epiphany festivals. Man's tragedy is that he seeks after lesser lights, instead of the Light. Even the symbols of Epiphany—Wise Men and the Star—can become an end in themselves, thus obscuring the Christ to whom these symbols point. Again and again, men need to be confronted with the words of Jesus Christ: "I am the light of the world; he who follows me will not walk in darkness, but will have the light of life."

Now, this is a fantastic claim to make, one which is a stumbling block to those who believe that Christ is a light among lights shoulder to shoulder with Mohammed and Buddha. But Jesus said, "I am the light of the world," and the church from earliest times has proclaimed this as good news. The whole door of discovery swings on God's revelation in Christ. Alec Vidler recalls the traditional service of *Tenebrae,* which is held during Holy Week. In this service, a number of candles in a triangular-shaped candlestick are extinguished one by one, till only a single candle remains lighted at the top. The whole rest of the church is in darkness. He then quotes this striking paragraph by Father George Tyrrell:

> As at Tenebrae . . . one after another of the lights are extinguished, till one alone—and that the highest of all—is left, so it is often with the soul and her guiding stars. In our early days, these are many—parents, teachers, friends, books, authorities—but, as life goes on, one by one they fail and leave us in deepening darkness, with an increasing sense of the mystery and inexplicability of all things, till at last none but the figure of Christ stands out luminous against the prevailing night.[2]

The God in Christ confronts us not as a partial claim to our loyalty, but as a disturbing absolute, a "divine imperative," an "either/or." This is not to say that there is no truth apart from knowledge of Jesus Christ, for certainly there is a light that enlightens every man. Still, wherever there is truth, wherever there is light, wherever there is true humanity, Christians humbly confess that Christ is present whether he is recognized or not.

> Our little systems have their day;
> They have their day and cease to be:
> They are but broken lights of thee,
> And thou, O Lord, art more than they.[3]

Consider how Jesus Christ lights the world. Western civilization is inexplicable without reference to this

Jewish teacher who never wrote a book and who never left his own small country. He has so profoundly affected our behavior that even men who have forgotten his name champion the very causes to which his teachings gave birth. "Live as though you were a legislator for the whole human race!" cries the atheist Sartre, as he underlines personal responsibility. But he writes against the backdrop of the Christian faith, with some of his own valuable insights coming from Christian thinkers such as Kierkegaard and Kant. Hospitals, schools, fair employment acts, self-determination for nations, abolition of slavery, civil rights, and relief for the poor find their root in Jesus Christ.

Are we not also aware of the impact of Christ on the world's great music? The first beginnings of polyphonic music came from the Christian liturgy. We possess harmony, part-singing—yes, even the popular music of the jukebox—because of the influence of Christian worship. And think of how greatly impoverished the treasury of Western music would be without Handel's *Messiah,* Bach's *Mass in B Minor,* Hayden's *The Creation,* Mozart's *Requiem,* and Britten's *A Ceremony of Carols.*

Our literature is dependent upon Christ for its greatest themes and clearest insights. In poetry, Christ has influenced Dante, Milton, Browning, T. S. Eliot, W. H. Auden, and Dylan Thomas. Without the Christian tradition, great novels such as Dickens' *Christmas Carol,* Dostoevski's *The Brothers Karamazov,* Hawthorne's *The Scarlet Letter,* Melville's *Moby Dick,* Steinbeck's

East of Eden, and Camus' *The Fall* could never have been written.

Every day we breathe, whether we acknowledge it or not, we are constantly affected in our social, political, economic, and cultural life by Jesus Christ. We cannot even date a letter without reference to a system of calculating time based on his advent. "His name," said Emerson, "is not so much written as ploughed in history."

Still Christians know that what we have so far attributed to Jesus Christ is merely the "fallout" from his major work—his purpose of reconciling mankind to God. Jesus Christ came on a divine rescue mission to free man from darkness and death and to bring him to light and life. A friend of mine said once that the difference between a good and a bad theologian was that the good theologian recognized the doctrines that were existential, that is, gripping the whole man in his life-situation. Jesus Christ is existential. He does not come to some other man; he comes to each of us. He confronts us with the truth about ourselves and shows us that our deepest need is answered only by him. He offers us his Self in a dynamic personal encounter that radically changes the course of our lives, bringing healing to our sickness, reconciliation to our estrangement, and hope to our despair.

Epiphany has been called the season of the star. And this star points to even a greater light, Jesus Christ, and to a lively possibility: "He who follows me will not walk in darkness but shall have the light of life." Christ shares his power with us. The demonic forces—estrangement, meaninglessness, death—no longer pose any real threat to us. We will always battle them, of course, but the victory is assured in advance because he who is the Light of the World has done battle with evil and has brought everlasting light to shine in the darkness.

As you receive the bread and cup today, I pray that you may have the darkness of your life dispelled by the One who is light and you may arise from this table to walk forever in his radiancy.

Lent

THE LORD'S DEATH

I Cor. 11:26

The long shadow of the cross falls over every observance of Holy Communion. Paul said, "For as often as you eat this bread and drink the cup, you proclaim the Lord's death until he comes." This is especially true during Lent, when the season as well as the sacrament proclaims the Lord's death. The liturgical color for Lent is purple, symbolizing penitence and preparation. The church considers the life of Jesus in a special way —his wilderness temptations, his teachings, his obedience, particularly his death and passion. On Ash Wednesday, we begin the long pilgrimage toward Jerusalem and Calvary; on Palm Sunday, we rejoice in a temporary triumph; during Holy Week, we recall events which move to the tragic climax on Good Friday. Then, we kneel in adoration before the cross, meditating on the Lord's death.

Still, we call this sacrament the Eucharist, which means "thanksgiving," and we sing hymns of praise during Lent. Why? Because through the Lord's death, hollow men are able to become whole. It is the supreme revelatory event of the ages, carving in history the truth about man and the truth about God.

The Lord's death reveals the depths of man's sin. The crucifixion of Jesus was brutal, ugly, cruel, showing man at his worst. The persecutors of Jesus were not pawns on a gigantic chessboard used by God to fulfill his purpose. They were free men who made free choices. Around Calvary, the scene was filled with grimacing faces of hate. Angry fists shook at the lonely figure on the cross. Venomous words swirled around him: " 'You who would destroy the temple and build it in three days, save yourself! If you are the Son of God, come down from the cross. . . . He saved others; he cannot save himself. He is the King of Israel; let him come down now from the cross, and we will believe in him' " (Matt. 27:40, 42). Jesus Christ died, and his enemies at the foot of the cross were glad. Their eyes, blinded by sin, could not see that the scripture had been fulfilled. For them, Jesus was an evil man and they had done the right thing by quickly disposing of him.

It would be a relief if we could regard the Lord's death as a past event, for then we could express our righteous indignation against evil men who put him to death and utter inane stupidities about how if we had been there, things would have been different. "We wouldn't have stood by!" we say. The fact is that we cannot regard the Lord's death in the past tense; the cross is contemporary. One of the Negro spirituals has a haunting refrain, "Were you there when they crucified my Lord?" Of course, we were there. And we do not stand by; we actively participate in crucifying Jesus Christ. We are guilty of the same sins that crucified Jesus. We are there in the bitter betrayal of Judas; we are there in the fearful silence of the disciples; we are there in the self-righteousness of the Pharisees; we are there in the cynical compromise of Pilate; we are there in the blind loyalty of the Roman soldiers to earthly authority.

We do not want to see what the cross reveals about ourselves. We flee from it like death; indeed, this truth does spell death for us. We are sinners, guilty men, crucifiers of the Christ. Willfully we have separated ourselves from God in an effort to become God. And when he sends grace and truth to us in Jesus Christ, we kill him. Bitter though this revelation is, the word of judgment is necessary before the good news about God makes any sense. The cross is a mirror in which we may see ourselves and, although it is an ugly, twisted reflection, this view points to man's greatest need: the forgiving love of God. We must bow our heads in confession and contrition before we can lift our voices in praise and thanksgiving.

Praise and thanksgiving! Eucharist! This mood prevails as we proclaim the Lord's death because the cross reveals not only the depths of man's sin, but also the depths of God's love. The bad news of man's sin is overcome by the good news of God's love.

There is another face on Golgotha's hillside. The face of Jesus Christ is filled with pain and suffering and love. He who overcame temptations in the wilderness overcame temptations to save himself on the cross. He hung there, helpless and weak. "Father, forgive them; for they know not what they do," he prayed. And as he died, "Father, into thy hands I commit my spirit!" The life, death, and resurrection of Jesus Christ convinced his followers of *God's* love. Jesus' crucifixion was not like Socrates drinking the hemlock, or Joan of Arc burning at the stake. His death was not a martyrdom, the bad end of a good man. It had revelatory significance, which pointed beyond the man Jesus to the very structures of reality, to God. Men stand at the foot of the cross, and say, "God so loved the world that he gave his only Son, that whoever believes in him should not perish but have eternal life" (John 3:16).

The depths of man's sin are met by the depths of God's love. The cross of Jesus Christ shows God bearing the awful consequences of sin. God takes sin seriously, for he is the holy God. He does not pass lightly over sin like an indulgent grandfather in heaven. This is a moral universe, and it is ordered so that sin causes suffering. God wants man to be reconciled to him. This purpose is not achieved without tremendous cost. God's forgiveness is neither easy nor cheap. Because he takes our sin seriously, his forgiveness is not a matter of easy routine, but of suffering love. And could it be any other way? If God's forgiveness were easy, would it have any power to free us to newness of life? Would a cheap love call forth our faith and devotion? Of course not!

E. Stanley Jones tells a story which illustrates the meaning of God's action in the crucifixion. There was a man who had a beautiful and intelligent wife. He was faithful to her until he was away from her on a business venture. It was then that he began his infidelity and he continued in this course after he had returned home. His wife's trust and faith in him were more than he could stand and he felt he must tell her what he had done. He feared her anger, and was afraid, also, that she might leave him. But at last, he told her.

"I can never forget," he said, "the look of anguish that came over her face as the meaning of what I had done dawned upon her. She turned pale, and clutching at the pain in her heart, she sank upon the bed. I could see my sin torturing her. Then she rose and I expected the storm to break upon me, but instead she said, 'I love you still and I will not leave you.' "

"Then," he said, "I saw in the anguished love of my wife the meaning of the cross. From her love I stepped up to the cross. I was a redeemed man from that hour."

Forgiveness, when it is real, is never easy. The wife had been wronged, and she took the hurt of separation into herself. Because she loved her husband deeply, he was capable of hurting her deeply. Her forgiveness was possible only through the pain of bearing with his sin. In a more profound way, this is the way it is with God. We have hurt him because we have willfully separated ourselves from him. He takes this hurt into himself, bears the suffering caused by our sin, and forgives us in an extremely costly way. Whenever God forgives, there is a cross.

The cross of Jesus Christ digs down deep in the earth —to the very foundations. As we meditate upon the Lord's death, we are driven to see the depths of our sin. But what joy divine! God, in his mercy, uses the Lord's death to free us from our sin. Here we see a love that will not let us go, a love that seeks us wherever we go, a love that bears all things.

> See, from his head, his hands, his feet,
> Sorrow and love flow mingled down:
> Did e'er such love and sorrow meet,
> Or thorns compose so rich a crown? [1]

Eastertide

NOT A FUNERAL SERVICE!

The Lord's Supper is not a funeral service! Usually we observe the sacrament as if we were in deep mourning—an air of absolute gloom hangs over the service like London fog. We sing hymns half-heartedly, mumble the ritual unintelligibly, drag our feet somberly to the table, and, generally, look as though we were at a funeral service of a good friend or close relative.

I am convinced that part of our problem stems from an overemphasis on the memorial idea of the Lord's Supper. In explaining the sacrament, we fall into the trap of speaking about its significance in the past tense. Surely, there is truth in the memorial interpretation of the Lord's Supper. All churches regard memory as an important aspect of its meaning. Christians are incurably historical in nature, and we look back to actual historical occurrences—Incarnation, Crucifixion, and

Resurrection. Were it not for the event of Jesus of Nazareth bursting into time and splitting it in two, there would be no church and, of course, no sacraments. Yes, remembering sacred history is vital to faith.

At the same time, this memorial interpretation of the sacrament is only a half-understanding. To interpret the Lord's Supper as only a memorial means a barren sacrament, void of life and reality. If the Lord's Supper is merely a memorial meal, then the modern day disciples of Jesus Christ gather to remember that Jesus Christ once suffered, died, and was resurrected, rather than encounter him as a present reality. Such an observance would be on the same order as a group of friends gathering on the birthday of a departed colleague to speak about his life and its meaning for them. That's fine, but their friend isn't with them.

In one way or another, the church has always affirmed belief in what the theologians call the Real Presence. This understanding has not always been clearly explained, nor has it been entirely satisfactory to everyone. Still, the doctrine of the Real Presence has been carefully preserved in the Protestant tradition. The doctrine means simply that those who take this sacrament in faith find Christ as truly present to them spiritually as the bread and wine is to them physically. The hymn writer expressed the feeling of millions of Christians when he wrote:

> Here, O my Lord, I see Thee face to face,
> Here would I touch and handle things unseen,

Here grasp with firmer hand eternal grace,
And all my weariness upon Thee lean. . . .

Too soon we rise: the symbols disappear;
The feast, though not the love, is past and gone;
The bread and wine remove: but Thou art here,
Nearer than ever—still my shield and sun.[1]

We don't gather just to remember the historical Jesus. The church is not built on the historical Jesus, but on the Risen Christ. The Lord's Supper is the joyous banquet of a Risen Lord who discloses himself to the church in every present moment. The Real Presence of God in the sacrament is a logical consequence of his resurrection.

In John Mansfield's play, *The Trial of Jesus,* Procula asks the centurion about the crucified Jesus: "Do you think he's dead?" "No, lady, I don't," was his startling reply. "Then where is he?" she asked. "Let loose in the world, lady, where neither Roman nor Jew can stop his truth." He is loose in the world. The cross could not capture him. The grave could not imprison him. He is loose in the world.

Jesus Christ said concerning his Supper, "Do this in remembrance of me." The word translated remembrance is *anamnesis* in the original Greek and, according to some scholars, it is not faithfully represented in our English word "remembrance." Our word suggests something which is absent and only mentally recollected. In the Scriptures, this Greek word *anamnesis* and its cognate verb have the sense of "re-calling" or representing before God an event in the past so that it becomes here and now a living reality. So, a better translation of the command of Jesus is: "Do this for my re-calling." When we celebrate this sacrament, Jesus Christ stands among us and the power of his presence pervades our personalities.

The story of the crucifixion-resurrection can be summed up in one word: running. When the disciples saw Jesus arrested, they ran for their lives out of the garden and into the night. Peter, the strong, second in command to Jesus, denied his Lord three times. The other disciples fled and hid. According to the earliest Gospels, none of the disciples were near the hill of the skull. Jesus was left, helpless, to die alone with the jeers of his detractors ringing in his ears.

"Peter, Peter, why are you running away?"
"They have crucified my Lord!"
"Peter, Peter, don't you love him enough to stay?"
"I am afraid."
"Peter, Christ will give you courage!"
"My dreams are destroyed. There is no hope."
"Peter, don't run, don't run . . . stay . . ."

Then, something happens. We cannot explain it logically or scientifically. The event is to be seen only by the eyes of faith. The disciples are running again—to the tomb where Jesus was laid. And it is empty. They are afraid, astonished, amazed. They are not sure what has happened. But it dawns upon them that Christ is alive. They run from the tomb to spread the good news to all his followers.

"Peter, Peter, why are you running away?"
"I am not running away; I am running toward."
"Aren't you afraid, Peter?"
"What is there to be afraid of? The Lord is Risen!"

What a change! One hundred and eighty degrees about face. The band of Jesus' men, discouraged and divided, running in all directions for fear of their lives, were suddenly united in the power of the resurrection faith and were running in all directions to spread the Gospel.

The Lord is risen! He is risen indeed! And his Presence makes the difference today as it did in ancient Jerusalem. David Livingstone once addressed a group of students at Glasgow University. When he stood to speak, the students saw a man who bore the scars of his African struggle. Haggard and thin, he was mute evidence of severe illnesses. His left arm, crushed by a lion, hung limp at his side. After describing his trials, he said, "Would you like me to tell you what supported me through all the years of exile among people whose language I could not understand and whose attitude toward me was always uncertain and often hostile? It was this: 'Lo, I am with you always, even unto the end of the world!' On those words I staked everything, and they never failed."

When you come to the Lord's table today, don't come looking into yourself and trying miraculously to "have faith." Come realizing that the Lord Jesus Christ is actually present. Truly, it is he that awakens faith within us and sustains us in the faith. When you come to the Lord's table today, know that Christian experience is not dependent upon you so much as it is upon God's action in Jesus Christ. Faith is not another burden imposed on the rest of our burdens, but a freeing of all burdens. "Come to me, all who labor and are heavy-laden, and I will give you rest."

The Lord's Supper is not a funeral service! We are not gathered to remember a dear departed leader. We are here to worship a Risen Lord in spirit and in truth. The resurrection joy leaps from every sentence of the ritual for the Lord's Supper. Perhaps it throbs through the *Sursum Corda* best of all:

> *Lift up your hearts.*
> We lift them up unto the Lord.
> *Let us give thanks unto the Lord.*
> It is meet and right so to do.

Confirmation
"THE WHOLE ARMOR OF GOD"
Eph. 6:11-17

There is an undeniable thrill about being a soldier. Think of the adventure of travel, the excitement of battle, and the mystery of secret mission. Some years ago a friend in the army wrote me saying that he was on a secret mission. All he could say was that he had just arrived in Mombasa after a twenty-four-day cruise across the Atlantic through the Mediterranean, the Suez Canal and the Red Sea. While in port, he traveled to Kilimanjaro, Zanzibar, and Nairobi. What a way to sight-see, with Uncle Sam picking up the tab!

But this not a recruitment speech for the U.S. Army. I want to speak about being a Christian soldier. Now perhaps you don't like to hear it put this way! Some shudder to hear Christianity described in military metaphors. They say, "Christianity is a religion of peace, not war. Armies are brutal, killing and maiming. The church has nothing in common with an army." However, Christian history shows that military metaphors have long been used. Paul sounded the trumpet call to discipleship in this way: "Put on the whole armor of God, that you may be able to stand against the wiles of the devil." And when Christians sought to describe baptism and the Lord's Supper, they attached the name, sacrament. This word sacrament comes from the Latin word *sacramentum,* which refers to the oath a Roman soldier took to his commander and his country. As the Roman soldier made this sacred oath to risk everything for his nation, so Christian soldiers pledge themselves to God and his kingdom when they observe the Lord's Supper.

Let us look at this armor of God. There is truth for a belt, righteousness for a breastplate, peace for shoes, faith for a shield, salvation for a helmet, and the word of God for a sword. These qualities are the Christian's fighting equipment which he must have to do war against principalities, powers, the rulers of darkness in this world, spiritual wickedness in high places.

Like so many of life's valuables, the armor of God was laid out for us before we were born. It is the same armor that patriarchs, prophets, apostles, and saints wore. And you can be certain that the armor of God is not given us because we deserve it. Deliver us from Jack Horner Christianity!

Little Jack Horner
Sat in the corner,
Eating a Christmas pie:
He put in his thumb,
And he took out a plum,
And said, "What a good boy am I!"

Christian faith will have nothing to do with such insufferable pride. God's armor is laid out for us because we are undeserving, because we are sinners who need his help more than anything else. God's undeserved grace to us is the fundamental proclamation of the Christian gospel.

The God whom we worship and our response is most dramatically symbolized in the sacrament of infant baptism. The baby—often crying and sometimes sleeping, always ignorant of what is happening—is brought to the altar and baptized with water into the faith. Baptism is the church's affirmation in "visible words" that the nature of God is to seek man before we seek him. "In this is love, not that we loved God, but that he loved us" (I John 4:10*a*). God's love confronts us at the center of life. He loves us whether we love him or not. His love is not dependent upon a "proper" response. All of this is symbolized by the sacrament of infant baptism. And more. For we see in this sacrament that the style of the Christian life is to receive from God's hands and to praise him for his freely given gifts. We do not have to be aggressive or demanding toward God, for our relationship, as Alan Richardson has said, is that of "a lover waiting at the trysting-place (rather) than that of a general storming a citadel."

There is also another side to wearing God's armor. Although this armor is laid out for us and we do not deserve to put it on, we are called to wear it. God has decided for us, and we must also decide for him. His love comes to us; we are called to love him in return. Christian discipleship is a summons to decision, and our baptism as infants is incomplete until we come back to the altar as responsible persons and confirm what was done at our baptisms.

You were born into a certain household, with a father and mother, perhaps brothers and sisters. You could not change this fact. Yet as you grew older and gained ability to make your own decisions, you could either accept or deny your home. There came a time when you could run away like the prodigal son in Jesus' parable. The same is true of your life in the church. You cannot change the fact of your infant baptism. But you have the freedom to deny or affirm the household of faith into which you were born.

Christian life is not easy; it is hard. To become a Christian is not to retire behind the lines to safety, but to be thrust into the very thick of battle. Christian faith has always produced martyrs—men who were not afraid to die for what they had lived for. It was only because they put on the whole armor of God, only because they had been possessed by the spirit of God, that they could courageously lay down their lives.

The age of martyrdom is not over. If we wear the whole armor of God today, we will experience rejection, persecution, and perhaps even death. Take the case of Jack Shea, once a successful vice-president of an oil company in Dallas, Texas. Shortly after the assassination of President Kennedy, Jack Shea wrote an article for *Look* magazine. It was a thoughtful analysis of Dallas' problems, looking through the confusion toward the future. He took precaution to speak as a private citizen, not as an official of his company. Even so, his company instituted a "gag rule" in response to outside pressure. He must agree not to comment publicly without formally clearing each word in advance and in writing. Not willing to go along with such a rule, Shea resigned. He said: "You don't sign away your citizenship for pay. The company policy reached beyond business into personal belief. I would have been promising never to exercise the right and responsibility of a citizen." [1] In addition to losing his company position, Shea was flooded with hate letters, accused in Far Right literature of aiding communism, and ostracized by old "friends."

Consider, too, the Christians who founded Koinonia Farm in Americus, Georgia. For over fifteen years, they have lived together as a close-knit community. They improved farming techniques, sharing the knowledge with the whole area. They loaned money to struggling neighbors. Still, the community came under fire because it was an interracial fellowship. Some of the Koinonia adults were excommunicated from their local churches in Americus. Their roadside fruit and vegetable stands were dynamited. Raiding parties rode into their yard and shot at houses. No one would sell fertilizer or supplies to them; no local outlets would help them market their goods. For a long time, Koinonia's Negro families were forced to leave out of consideration for their children's safety. Those committed Christians were branded as communists by the Georgia legislature, persecuted by their neighbors, and denied protection of law.

Søren Kierkegaard once wrote:

> It is very dangerous to go into eternity with possibilities one has oneself prevented from becoming realities. A possibility is a hint from God. One must follow it. In every man there is latent the highest possibility, one must follow it. . . . Trusting to God I have dared, but I was not successful; in that is to be found peace, calm, and confidence in God. I have not dared: that is a woeful thought, a torment in eternity.[2]

Real Christianity is not pedestrian. Real Christianity is not safe and secure. The Christian steadfastly refuses to be squeezed into the world's mold, but is transformed by God's will. It takes daring to be a Christian, for a Christian is under fire from front and behind.

God offers us the possibility of becoming Christian.

I dare you today to accept this possibility. I challenge you to live as a good soldier of Jesus Christ. Confirm in this service what was done at your baptism. As you take bread and wine to your lips, pledge yourself anew to Christ the King. "Put on the whole armor of God, that you may be able to stand against the wiles of the devil" (Eph. 6:11).

Pentecost

FOUR ROOMS

Come with me back in time, back nearly two thousand years. I want to take you on a tour of some rooms that are etched forever in the memory of Christians. They are important, not because they are elaborate, but because our Lord Jesus Christ filled the places with his presence. Whenever Christians gather to worship, the events which transpired in these rooms are preached about and celebrated.

First, there is an upper room in Jerusalem. Climb the steps; stand beside the door; look inside. A group of men are eating a meal, quietly, even solemnly. Much of the room is wrapped in shadows, and it is hard to make out the figures. Yet if we look closely, we can see that it is the prophet from Nazareth, Jesus, and his disciples. It is evident that they are eating a Passover meal together. Before them are unleavened cakes, wine, water, bitter herbs, and a lamb brought from the Temple. This is a festival meal which Jewish rabbis took with their disciples, and recalls to mind the deliverance of the Jews from the Egyptians.

Still, this is more than a Passover meal. Jesus does a strange thing. He takes one of the round cakes of bread, gives thanks, and breaks it into pieces, passing them around the table. "Take, eat, this is my body," he commands. Then, he takes the cup, gives thanks, and gives it to them to drink. He speaks again, "Drink of it, all of you; for this is my blood of the covenant, which is poured out for many for the forgiveness of sins."

The disciples are completely mystified. They do not know what to think, and are uncomfortable at their Master's words. They never could understand his saying that he would have to suffer and die. And by giving them bread and wine in this way, he proclaims with powerful symbols that this is precisely what he must do. Instead of being crowned with a golden crown as the deliverer of Jews from Roman hands, he will be crowned with thorns and die a humiliating death.

Whenever we observe the Lord's Supper, we enter this upper room in Jerusalem, remembering that Jesus Christ has become the new Passover Lamb whose blood is spilled to ratify God's new covenant with his people.

There is a second room, located in Emmaus. It is Sunday, the first day of the week. Into the room come three travelers. Two of them are disciples of Jesus, Cleopas and perhaps his wife. The other traveler—unknown to either of them—is the resurrected Christ. The disciples ask their strange companion to stay with them, since night is drawing near. On the road, they had told him about Jesus, how he died, and the rumors about his resurrection. And he had "interpreted to them in all the scriptures the things concerning himself." Still, they do not recognize him until the evening meal. They sit down to eat an ordinary meal. Jesus, as in the upper room before his death, takes bread, blesses and breaks it, and gives it to them. In that instant, the disciples recognize him. He vanishes out of their sight. They speak to each other, "Did not our hearts burn within us while he talked to us on the road, while he opened to us the scriptures?" (Luke 24:32). Rising immediately, the two return to Jerusalem. There they learn that the Risen Lord had appeared to Simon, and they excitedly tell how he was known to them in the breaking of bread.

In the first room, Jesus speaks of his approaching death. In the second room at Emmaus, the disciples see their Lord triumphant over death. This meal is a joyous banquet which the Messiah celebrates with his disciples. Is it only an accident that their eyes are opened when Jesus breaks bread? I think not. Countless millions have had their eyes opened to the joy of resurrection as they joined in the Eucharist. Death and Resurrection, Defeat and Triumph are fused together in this meal.

Now, let us journey back to Jerusalem to see the third

room. No one knows for sure where it was located, although some believe that it was the same upper room in which Jesus had his last meal with the disciples. Even so, after the Crucifixion and Resurrection, this is a different room filled with different men. The day is Pentecost, the Jewish festival which marked the close of the grain harvest. The disciples have gathered in this room. Suddenly, without warning, a sound comes from heaven like the rush of a mighty wind. The disciples are seized by the experience of a Presence; tongues of fire—symbolizing power—rest on their heads. They are filled with the Holy Spirit and begin to speak in other tongues.

In this room, the Christian Church was born. The coming of the Holy Spirit meant the coming of a new community, a new Israel, constituted by the death and resurrection of Jesus Christ. At Pentecost as at Emmaus, Christ made himself known to his disciples. The Holy Spirit is none other than the God who sent Jesus Christ into the world pouring out a great blessing on his people, making known that he is with us even to the end of the world.

Remember what happened after this Pentecost experience? The disciples went from this room into all the world, obedient to their Lord's command. Those men who were afraid to watch him die on the cross were given the power to march against Rome—which must have appeared as a mouse doing battle with a cat —and to win. J. B. Phillips, in his preface to *The*

Young Church in Action, wrote, "It is a matter of sober historical fact that never before has any small body of ordinary people so moved the world that their enemies could say, with tears of rage in their eyes, that these men 'have turned the world upside down'!" [1] As we celebrate this Pentecost season, I hope that we can catch the zeal of those early Christians who were seized by God's Holy Spirit and literally thrown into the service of the world.

We have toured three rooms: the upper room where Jesus instituted the Lord's Supper in preparation for his death; the Emmaus room where Jesus revealed himself as the resurrected Lord; and the room where, at Pentecost, the disciples received the Holy Spirit. To tour the fourth room, we must return to the present.

Where is the fourth room located? It is here, right here, this very place where we have come to praise and thank God. It is here and it is also every room where Christians gather to remember Christ. And worship in this room today is vital to our Christian faith. What happens when we worship? Simply this: the there and then becomes the here and now! These past events in which God acted to redeem his people—Crucifixion, Resurrection, Pentecost—are recalled, indeed, reenacted. Like a sharp ray of light, the Christian past finds its focal point in one place, this place. The three rooms are set inside our one room, and we participate in events which free us to newness of life, thought, and action.

I don't know about you, but this is an absolutely exciting possibility for me. The most exciting possibility of life! For in this moment, in this room, we are brought into the presence of the Living God. It makes little difference about the externals of our worship. The sermon may be a terrible bore, the choir may sing off key, the organist may play the wrong chords, the ushers may be unfriendly. A hundred things may go wrong in the service, but one thing will always go right. God will be present. These historical occurrences will be made a reality through his Holy Spirit and, if we are open to him, we will leave this room as did the first disciples: changed men, charged with his Spirit, anxious to speak his word, thanking him for his great mercies.

> I'll praise my Maker while I've breath;
> And when my voice is lost in death,
> Praise shall employ my nobler powers:
> My days of praise shall ne'er be past,
> While life, and thought, and being last,
> Or immortality endures.[2]

Independence Sunday

UNLEAVENED BREAD

Ex. 12:39 Mark 14:22

The bread which Jesus took in his hands at the last supper was unleavened bread. This was a special meal, not only because it was the last he would eat with his disciples before his crucifixion and because during the meal he instituted the sacrament of the Lord's Supper, but also because it was the Passover meal. And the Passover, for the Jews, was like the Fourth of July for us. It was a national holiday, or to use the word as it should be used, a holy day. The Passover celebration marked the deliverance of the Hebrew people from the oppressive power of Egypt.

At the Passover meal, the bread was unleavened for a purpose. The children of Israel ate the Passover as their forefathers had done—poised for flight. The book of Exodus gives us insight into what happened. As the

Hebrews were fleeing from the Egyptians, "they baked unleavened cakes of the dough which they had brought out of Egypt, for it was not leavened, because they were thrust out of Egypt and could not tarry, neither had they prepared for themselves any provisions" (Ex. 12: 39). There was no time to wait leisurely for the yeast to work, for the enemy would soon be breathing fire down their necks.

The first thing unleavened bread brings to mind on this Sunday before Independence Day is this: the bread which Jesus took symbolized a political occurrence. For the Hebrews, the Exodus was a sign of God's gracious activity toward them. It was his mighty act by which he sealed their deliverance from the hands of the enemy. This was celebrated, not merely in the synagogue, but in all Jewish society. To those who claim that politics and religion must be kept separate, the only sensible reply is: How? The Hebrews were much more intelligent than some Christians at this point. There is no word in Hebrew for "religion." Religion was not a part of life; it was life itself. Religion can never be a department; it is a stance that illuminates all of one's relationships.

And what of the new reality which the bread was to symbolize? "Take, eat, this is my body," Jesus said. The crucifixion was not a religious act. The cross was not raised in the serene beauty of a sanctuary, but stuck in the black earth of a windswept hillside known as Golgotha—the place of the skull. The crucifixion was a secular occurrence having political significance. The Apostles' Creed tells us that Jesus was put to death under Pontius Pilate. Jesus shouldered his cross because he stood in the prophetic tradition which refused to sugarcoat bitter injustice with sweet platitudes about God's love. All of man's misery, heartache, and pain were of deep concern to him. He did not come to bring peace, but a sword. And the sword cut deep into the social customs of his day.

Christians must take their responsibilities in the world more seriously. George Bernard Shaw once likened a modern church congregation to a mob of hermits coming to fill their cups at a well and then carrying them back to their caves. Often, pathetically enough, this is not an unfair observation. We are involved in busy work in the church while great social evils go unchecked. Our churches resemble giant fallout shelters where we try to hide from serving the world. We need to come out of our fallout shelters. Informed Christians should be in the world, working in political parties, community projects, and places of greatest need, earnestly seeking the mind of Christ.

Rufus Jones, the Quaker philosopher, wrote about the Evangelical movement in the eighteenth century of which the Wesleys were an important part:

> The most remarkable thing about it was the freshly inspired social impulse which it produced. It reformed prisons, it stopped the slave trade, it freed slaves. It made its

converts uncomfortable over wrong social conditions. It sent missionaries to create hospitals and to conquer ignorance in almost every land on the globe. It was always as much outward as it was inward.[1]

Christianity is always as much outward as inward. The gospel has always resulted in social and political change when men have had the courage to face its implications.

Unleavened bread also suggests a willingness to forego luxuries in order to reach fundamental goals. "Leave the leaven behind! We don't have time for the bread to rise!" This was the cry of the Hebrews as they packed the necessities of life for the escape from Egypt.

Americans are yeast-lovers. The enemy is at the door, crisis is upon us, the sand is running low in the top of the hourglass. Still, we leisurely take our ease in Zion, not marking the signs of the times. We have become more interested in obtaining the luxuries of our technological age than reaching the goals on which our country was founded. Ours is the affluent society where people worry about losing weight while most of the world's population worry about getting enough food to stay alive. Our median income is seven thousand dollars a year compared with an average annual income in India of fifty dollars. We promote planned obsolescence. Dennis Brogan characterized modern Americans as people "who go away and leave things." The old is never good enough; we are constantly searching for the new.

A good index to our pleasure-oriented character is how we spend our money. We criticize the government for wasteful spending, but what about private spending? In one year, Americans spent $193 per capita on liquor; almost three billion dollars for movies and recreation; seven billion for furs, jewelry, and gambling; ten billion for cosmetics; and the paltry sum of nine hundred million for all churches and charities. Americans spend more money a year on expensive funerals than on educating youth. We are not living under the sense of urgency; we are living as if we have all the time in the world.

We think that hard-won liberty is easily kept. We believe that because the nation has produced great heroes like Washington, Lincoln, and Lee, we can afford to be cowards and never stick our necks out for a cause bigger than our pocketbooks. But listen to Goethe: "What you have inherited from your fathers, earn over again for yourselves or it will not be yours." Being free is not the same as being free and easy. Continued freedom demands that we learn the lessons of the past and discipline ourselves for the challenges of the future. Our national inheritance must be won again every day; we cannot live on our fathers' good names.

"Simplicity, simplicity, simplicity!" thundered Thoreau. "I say, let your affairs be as two or three, and not a hundred or a thousand; instead of a million count half a dozen, and keep your accounts on your thumbnail." Someone will immediately point out the impossibility of returning to a Walden II and, of course, we cannot. Yet we can simplify our lives, cutting out the excess, trimming down the luxuries, directing our energies toward a "loftier race." The yeast of life—luxury—is nice, but it will be dust in our mouths if we forget the one thing needful for a healthful nation: dedication to the God who holds our history in his hands, and a subsequent labor for liberty and justice for all.

Labor Sunday

HOLY COMMUNION AND WORK

I Cor. 10:31

What have Holy Communion and work in common? It seems incongruous to speak of them in the same breath. Are they not as far apart as east from west? Work is soiled and smudged with the sweat of daily grind; Holy Communion is set aside on a white cloth. Work takes place in the world, hustling and bustling; Holy Communion is administered in the church, quietly and solemnly. Work has to do with gold; Holy Communion speaks of God. These are probably our first reactions to the idea.

But no! Holy Communion and work are inexorably connected. Life cannot be neatly divided into categories of sacred and secular. "It is a mistake," wrote Archbishop William Temple, "to suppose that God is primarily interested in religion." God is primarily interested in everything. He is the Creator; nothing was made without his hand. He participates fully in his entire creation, thus erasing any distinction between sacred and secular. What happens outside church—in the smoke factory, the sweat of mine, the smell of bakery—is as important to God as what goes on inside church. The church is not an island of sacredness surrounded by a pagan sea. God, in Christ, has claimed all of life for himself.

We have become so accustomed to Holy Communion celebrated in the church building apart from the world that we cannot imagine it has anything vital to say about our work. This was not always so. The sacrament was first observed in an upper room of a Jewish home. Probably at the same time that, upstairs, Jesus took bread and wine in his hands, downstairs, dishes were being washed, a baby cried, and a man fed livestock. The early church always celebrated the Eucharist in homes because there were no church buildings. For a time, it was the climax to a common meal called the love feast. Church members would come and spread their meal—a kind of early covered dish supper—and, afterward, they would participate in the Lord's Supper as they sat at the table.

The early custom of home Communion has been recaptured in a parish in England which is set squarely in a crowded industrial area. The rector has established the custom of the congregation meeting in small groups in houses. Early on weekday mornings, there are house-church meetings with celebrations of Holy Communion. The kitchen table is moved to the living room of the dwelling. Used candles from the altar of the parish church are set on the table that becomes the altar. Homemade bread—the same bread the family ate for tea the night before—is used in the service. What is the reaction of those who have participated in the house Communion? They say: "I now feel that my house is really a bit of God's world," and "We find that we can't quarrel over the table at which Holy Communion has been celebrated." With the lunch box close to the Communion chalice, the relationship of worship and work is no longer foreign.

The symbols of bread and wine suggest the intimate relationship between Holy Communion and work. Bread and wine are parts of God's creation which have been worked on by man. The Lord's Supper means that work has been performed, for there can be no bread without baking and no wine without producing. Isn't it true that we have a difficult time finding God in man's production? Far easier to find God in nature, untouched by human hands! Usually when the church wants to challenge its members to deeper discipleship, it sponsors retreats to the country where we hear endless sermons on finding God in nature. The element of production seems to build a wall between God and man.

But the bread and wine of Communion proclaims joyously that the point of contact between God and man is not only unspoiled nature, but also our creativity. God encounters us in our work. God, as Creator, made man to imitate him, to join him in creating the world. Of course, this isn't all the story. Man, made in God's image, called to cooperate with God in creating, is fallen man. He has taken God's creation, twisted and distorted it in production. He has used the works of his hands, not to glorify God, but to glorify himself. "Glory be to man, for man is the master of things!" our machines seem to hum. The Doxology is noticeably absent from our industrial economy, and we teach our children that self-reliance in the Emersonian tradition is the highest virtue.

The reality of man's fall is met head-on in the Eucharist. For bread stands not simply for the goodness of God and the creative work of man; it stands for selfishness, exploitation, greed, class conflict, sin. Wine is the symbol of freedom and feast, but it is also a constant reminder of the depths to which man can sink in debauchery and drunkenness. Jesus knew this as he took the bread and wine. He knew that they were fallen products of a fallen world. But this did not stop him from saying over them, "This is my body . . . This is my blood." By doing this, he claimed all of life for the Kingdom and the new order which is to come. In Holy Communion, the false division between sacred and secular is abolished. The bread and wine, contaminated by human sin, is taken by Christ and consecrated. But nothing happens unless the power of sin over us is broken. And so, he takes the bread, blesses it, and breaks it. Then, he gives. He gives—not an idea, not a philosophy, not good advice—but he gives himself, completely, wholly, ultimately, for us. By his cross, he calls us back to our true selves, restores us to a right relationship with God, and consecrates us for service.[1]

Paul wrote to the Corinthians: "So, whether you eat or drink, or whatever you do, do all to the glory of God" (I Cor. 10:31). Whatever you do—whether you teach school or attend school, whether you work in an office or work in a field, whether you work with your hands or with your brains—do all to the glory of God. Our jobs—stained as they are by moral compromises—are nonetheless sacraments of service. As Luther said, "Our works are God's masks, behind which he does all things."

Can't you sense the excitement of this? When we do work that benefits the community, we cooperate with God in creation. No work—if it is done to the glory of God—is ever small or insignificant. Christ's hands touch bread and wine, and, behold, the bread and wine transcend themselves. God comes to us through them. Christ's hands touch our work, and, behold, it is lifted from the common to participate in the new reality. Listen to the personal testimony of a housewife:

One morning while working at a very routine household chore, my mind surged ahead relentlessly, like a tide engulfing me, revealing with great clarity, the meaning of

Christ's life, death, and Resurrection. It was a moment of illumination . . . In the cross, I found God. Purpose and meaning to life followed. . . . I was a small part of that omnipotent plan. In finding God I also found myself. . . .

In the days that followed, I felt as I had just emerged from a fog and I expected to see a dramatic change; a sharp contrast from black to white. I was disappointed. And yet was there a more subtle change? Now I was aware of my obligation to serve God and my fellow man. *I was keenly aware of the importance of all the mundane obscure events of my days, and the countless small omissions. It was significant to me that I had been working actively when I had this experience.*[2]

Someone has said, "Every Christian needs two conversions, first to Christ and then to the world." And Alec Vidler defined the Christian style of life as "holy worldliness." The goal of Christian living is not to retreat to a world of specifically religious activity inside the church and "let the rest of the world go by." It is to participate fully in life, witnessing to Christ where we live and work. This means there should perhaps be less work *in* the church (which is often "busy work") and more work *for* the church—out where people live and die. A baker was once asked what church work he did. He replied, "I bake." He had real insight into what we mean when we speak of Christian vocation.

Holy Communion and work. What have the two in common? Everything! And we dare not speak of them in separate breaths. Work, like Communion, is sacred.

When we realize this, life will take on a deeper dimension. We will take Communion in a different way, and we will do our work in a different way. G. A. Studdert-Kennedy, that masterful poet-preacher of another generation, captured the truth about the intimate relationship when he wrote:

> When through the whirl of wheels, and engines humming,
> Patiently powerful for the sons of men,
> Peals like a trumpet promise of His coming,
> Who in the clouds is pledged to come again;
>
> When through the night the furnace fires aflaring,
> Shooting out tongues of flame like leaping blood
> Speak to the heart of Love, alive and daring,
> Sing of the boundless energy of God.
>
> When in the depths the patient miner striving,
> Feels in his arms the vigor of his Lord,
> Strikes for a kingdom and his King's arriving,
> Holding his pick more splendid than the sword;
>
> When on the sweat of labor and its sorrow,
> Toiling in twilight flickering and dim,
> Flames out the sunshine of the great tomorrow,
> When all the world looks up because of Him—
>
> Then will He come with meekness for His glory,
> God in a workman's jacket as before,
> Living again the eternal gospel story,
> Sweeping the shavings from His work-shop floor.[3]

World-wide Communion Sunday

"THE WHOLE WORLD IN HIS HANDS"

Ps. 24:1-2 John 3:16

A few years ago, an old Negro spiritual was high on the hit parade. You could hardly escape the tune. Driving in the car, you heard it on the radio. Drinking coffee at a café, it was likely to be played on a jukebox. And if you had teen-agers, you might have heard it on the hi-fi at home. We tapped our feet to the melody, and perhaps even sang along. The words were very simple, repeated over and again: "He's got the whole world in his hands." That shouldn't sound so big that we forget he's got us as individuals in his hands, too. The spiritual didn't forget. One of the verses went: "He's got you and me, brother, in his hands."

Whether you like jazzed-up Negro spirituals, or whether you like jazz or Negro spirituals at all, doesn't make any difference. The point is that this spiritual faithfully captured the basic biblical insights about God and his relationship to his world. And considering how some of our hymns fall short of good theology, I think this was quite an achievement! Where did the spiritual find its text? In the Old Testament, in the book of Psalms. Listen to the opening verses of Ps. 24:

> The earth is the Lord's and
> the fulness thereof,
> the world and those who dwell
> therein;
> for he has founded it upon the seas,
> and established it upon the rivers.

This idea of God-ownership gave the Hebrews a tremendous sense of security. It gave them a feeling of security about nature. Remember, the Hebrews believed in a three-story universe. When God created the earth, he separated the waters with our world. Below the earth there was water. Above the earth—kept back by a kind of inverted bowl called heaven—was more water. And it was God who kept the waters from meeting and destroying the inhabitants. God caused the regularity of the seasons; the rain, the sunshine came from him. He was no nature god! Nature didn't control him; he controlled nature. God was over and above his creation. This was a profound insight of the early Hebrews. Belief in God's ownership also gave the Hebrews a sense of security about their personal lives. As the owner of the world and the God who made covenant with his people, he caused things to happen. For men of Old Testament times, the Exodus from Egypt stood as the primary symbol of God's love for his people. He had saved them from slavery and planted their feet on the promised land. He had raised up leaders to guide the people: kings, priests, and prophets. No wonder the psalmist could full-throatedly sing God's praises! "He's got you and me, brother, in his hands." "The Lord is my shepherd, I shall not want."

God is no absentee owner. He is alive and active in history. Isn't this truth seen in Jesus Christ? In Jesus Christ, the whole drama of history comes to a crashing climax. Jesus Christ, as Karl Barth has said, is the "hinge of history." He is the way all other historical events are to be interpreted; locked in his life is the meaning of our lives. In Jesus Christ, we do not find a new God revealed; rather we find the same God who was present at the creation showing himself in an ultimate way. God is saying in Jesus Christ: "This is who I always was and always will be: a God of sacrificial love." The God who owns the earth is no tyrant. He is God for us, as Paul knew. Look at the cross of Christ! The cross, if we examine it aright, is a window. Through it we are able to look at God's nature and find that he is love. "For God so loved the world that he gave his only Son, that whoever believes in him should not perish but have eternal life." The owner of the world is also its Redeemer. He gives himself to sinful man in the form of a servant. A cross is planted in the soil of the earth, blood runs red on that soil, and life is never the same again. Can you doubt that God is love as you stand at the bottom of the cross looking into the face of the Crucified One? The hands that hold the whole wide world are pierced hands.

God's ownership of the world suggests something else. Since God is the owner of the world, man is only the steward. There cannot be two owners. In the sixteenth century, the pope divided the world between two powers: Spain and Portugal. Spain owned all the land on one side of a line; Portugal owned all the land on the other side. A neat trick. Unfortunately, it didn't work! The grass always looked greener on the other side of the pope's line. Think of the wars fought and the lives lost over the question of who owns what. But man owns nothing and he deserves nothing either. Man is a sinner, a rebel against God. God is the owner. He gives to man his days on the earth. We are here as trustees only. Whatever we have that is good comes from God's graciousness and not because we deserve it. Since we do not own the world, it is not ours to do with as we want. We must follow the will of the owner, showing ourselves to be responsible stewards. "He's got the whole world in his hands" and, as stewards, we've got the whole world in our hands, too. We're responsible, not only for the little speck of ground we call home, but also for all the world.

The trouble is that we have regarded the rest of the world as strange and alien, not the world for which

Christ died. We're like that five-year-old boy in a Dallas school. A music teacher was teaching the children a song in French. After drilling them in French for awhile, she suddenly sang the song in English. "What language am I singing in now?" she asked. The boy was ready with an answer. "In human," he replied. We've felt that we're more human than anyone else! Our missionary enterprise often has been a vain flaunting of American superiority instead of a humble sharing of the gospel.

This is World-wide Communion Sunday. Perhaps you can see how significant this Sunday is by remembering that Christianity began in a country which could be placed three times in South Carolina and twenty-six times in Texas. This faith knew no boundaries. It burst out of the confines of religion and tradition, turning the ancient world upside down. It spread across Europe, into Asia and Africa, and finally came to be planted on American soil. Today, with only a few exceptions, the Christian faith is found in every country on the earth. No other faith has been spread so widely. Christianity is a universal faith that embraces all men.

As we take the bread and wine, other people in other lands who are of different color and speak a foreign language will also be holding out their hands. Our mission—the mission of the whole church—has always been to the world. To the people who say, "Let's take care of our own here at home before we send missionaries to another place in the world," the gospel replies, "Where is 'here at home'? Christ said to 'go into all the world.' " The fact of the matter is that the people who are always talking about taking care of the home folks usually are the ones who aren't interested in taking care of anybody. I don't see them giving any more to help people in our country than they do abroad.

The Lord's table extends around the whole wide world. We can't cut it off at our national borders. The Lord's table doesn't belong to us, but to our Lord. And his invitation is for all. So, our number is greatly enlarged. Although separated by space, we are one in Spirit. All of us the world over are kneeling at the same table, united by the same Lord.

The Lord's Supper is a sacrament of sharing. *Don't ever forget that!* At the heart of this sacrament is the affirmation that God through Christ gives to us and that we must share with others. On his World-wide Communion Sunday, we share a sacred meal together. But this is not enough. Our participation in this sacrament must represent that we share all of life with our neighbors around the world. The bread and wine, symbols of God's ultimate sharing with us, must become symbols of our sharing with our neighbors. Let us share our love, understanding, concern, and material gifts with the world. The whole wide world is in his hands—and ours.

Thanksgiving

"HE . . . GAVE THANKS"

Matt. 26:27 KJV

Thanksgiving Day is upon us, a national holiday filled with joy and festivity. But, in a real sense, whenever Christians gather to celebrate Holy Communion, it is thanksgiving day. Jesus observed the Passover meal with his disciples, and he gave thanks over the meal. We may forget to give thanks before our meals, or it may become boring routine, but for Jesus, such thanksgiving was a sacred custom. The prayer was brief and moving in its simplicity: "Blessed art thou, O Lord our God, King of the World, who dost bring forth fruit from the earth."

From earliest times, the element of thanksgiving played a large role in the sacrament of Holy Communion. So much, in fact, that a common name for this sacrament is the Eucharist, a Greek word which means "thanksgiving." Charles Wesley almost always referred to the service as the Holy Eucharist, and John Wesley did so frequently. In the ritual itself, thanksgiving rises like a great shout. Sometimes the prayers in the service, beginning with "Lift up your hearts," and continuing through the Prayer of Consecration, are called "The Great Thanksgiving." Christians give thanks for God's mighty act in Jesus Christ, for his great offering for our salvation, and for the hope of glory. The element of praise and thanksgiving needs to be restored to our worship as well as to our lives. At least three things happen to us when we join the psalmist in saying,

> Bless the Lord, O my soul;
> and all that is within me,
> bless his holy name! (Ps. 103.1).

First, when we give thanks to God, we are freed from the prison of self-pity. Thanksgiving releases us from self-pity because it forces us to look at life in a new way. No longer are we alone; God is with us. Whatever has happened to us and whatever will happen to us is under his care. The person who has learned to thank God is able to praise him in shadow and sunlight, in trouble and triumph, in failure and success. He comes to realize that in God's economy all things ultimately work together for the good. "For everything [give] thanks," Paul admonished. There are really only two ways to live: pitying oneself or giving thanks to God.

Martin Rinkhart, author of that magnificent hymn of praise, "Now Thank We All Our God," was a Lutheran pastor during the horrible Thirty Years' War. He read the burial service over forty to fifty people a day. Of the eight thousand people who died during the war, his wife was among them. His German homeland was laid waste. But his response was thanksgiving, not self-pity. "Now Thank We All Our God" was born from a time of trial and suffering that could have broken Rinkhart's spirit had he not known how to thank God.

And what of another German pastor—Dietrich Bonhoeffer—who was imprisoned for resistance against Hitler? From his cell in a concentration camp, he wrote, read, and prayed. Hitler killed his body, but he could not touch his soul. Listen to this prayer, written from prison:

> O heavenly Father,
> I praise and thank thee
> For the peace of the night.
> I praise and thank thee for this new day.
> I praise and thank thee for all thy goodness
> and faithfulness throughout my life.
> Thou hast granted me many blessings;
> Now let me accept tribulation
> from thy hand.
> Thou wilt not lay on me more
> than I can bear.
> Thou makest all things work together for good
> for thy children.[1]

When we give thanks to God, our relationship to him is changed. How do you usually pray to God? Be honest, now! We usually pray when we want things. Instead of containing adoration, confession, intercession, and thanksgiving, prayer becomes a brief S.O.S. Basically our problem is that we are self-oriented, instead of God-oriented. We turn to God as a means to get what we want, and not to acknowledge him as the end of all our wanting. Augustine was right when he said, "Our hearts are restless until they rest in thee."

Christianity today lacks the prophetic spirit. We want redemption without judgment, resurrection without crucifixion. Christianity is considered important—not in itself—but for what it can do for us. Because "the family that prays together stays together," the church is a good place to go. We are told that we should read the Bible because it helps to solve emotional problems. And Christianity is presented as a great dam against the dark waters of Communism. Most of what we are told about Christianity puts the cart before the horse. We often begin and end with asking how God can serve us, while forgetting the only relevant question is how we can be obedient to God.

Thanksgiving changes our relationship with God from self-oriented to God-oriented. When we begin our prayers with "Give us this day our daily bread," instead of "hallowed be thy name," the emphasis is on us, not God. Significantly, Jesus began his model prayer with "Our Father, who art in heaven, hallowed be thy name." Praise first, petition later, is the prayer rule he followed.

When our relationship with God is changed, we are changed, too. Life becomes a doxology. Praising God—

thanking him for his great mercies—is the only way to pray, and to live. The God whom we praise and thank is radically unlike the god whom we merely ask for things. The god who is a heavenly waiter doesn't exist. He is an idol, powerless to give us anything. The God whom we praise and thank is God. He is Judge and Redeemer, the Holy One, who makes a total claim on our lives. When we give thanks to God, we have a healthy relationship with him—one which begins "hallowed be thy name," and ends: "for thine is the kingdom, and the power, and the glory, for ever."

Finally, when we give thanks to God, we are able to possess our possessions. Ironic, isn't it, that our possessions often possess us? We fool ourselves into thinking that we are in the driver's seat, but it is more often true, as Emerson observed, that things are in the saddle and ride mankind. How tragic is the man who is possessed by his possessions. For he becomes less than human. It is a law of life that we become like whatever we worship. If we worship lifeless things, we become like them: unresponsive, inanimate, impersonal, dead. When are we going to learn that *being* is more important than *having?*

How many people have sacrificed great talent, honesty, integrity, peace of mind, for material gain! I think of James Tyrone, head of the pitiful clan in Eugene O'Neill's *Long Day's Journey into Night.* Tyrone had sacrificed a brilliant acting career for a mess of pottage. He bought a play, made it a great financial success, but it ruined him as an actor. Always playing the same role year after year, he forgot what it was to take on other parts. When he finally discovered he needed to change, he had become slave to one role and no one would have him. Years later, the old man confessed to his son:

In 1874 when Edwin Booth came to the theater in Chicago where I was leading man . . . he said to our manager, "That young man is playing Othello better than I ever did!" That from Booth, the greatest actor of his day or any other! And it was true! And I was only twenty seven years old! As I look back on it now, that night was the high spot in my career. I had life where I wanted it! . . . But a few years later my good bad luck made me find the big money-maker . . . and then life had me where it wanted me.[2]

Is this your autobiography? Does life have you by the throat? Have your possessions enslaved you? Long ago, Nietzsche realized the danger of being owned: "Whoever possesses little is possessed by that much less: praised be a little poverty."

Thanksgiving to God delivers us from slavery to our possessions, for we recognize that they are not of ultimate value. Possessions are seen from a different perspective —not significant in themselves—but significant because they come from God. Indeed, our possessions can become reminders of his love toward us, and they can be regarded as potentially good because they are part of God's good creation.

Truly, this is a sacrament of praise and thanksgiving!

General Meditations

COME WITH FAITH

Two words are fundamental to Christianity: "come" and "faith." Jesus Christ was always issuing a glad invitation to discipleship. To the distressed and depressed, he said, "Come to me, all who labor and are heavy-laden, and I will give you rest" (Matt. 11:28). To the rich young ruler, his word was, "Come, follow me" (Matt. 19:21*b*). Scores turned away from his invitation, and no wonder. For his way was not easy; it demanded the whole man. "If any man would come after me, let him deny himself and take up his cross and follow me" (Matt. 16:24). The early church took his glad invitation and, preaching the good news to all men, asked them to "Come and see."

Coming by itself is not enough. Always, men are called to have faith. Jesus said simply, "Have faith in God" (Mark 11:22). For those who found healing for their bodies and spirits, it was always a result of faith.

"Your faith has made you well" (Matt. 9:22*b*). The great apostle of faith was Paul, who preached that man is found righteous before God by faith alone.

Men are encouraged to come to Jesus Christ, but they must come with faith. The invitation to the Lord's Supper contains the phrase "Draw near with faith." This is not only a requirement for taking the Lord's Supper; it is also necessary for a vital encounter with Jesus Christ.

What do we mean by "faith"? Faith, like love, is a confused word in the English language. One popular idea goes that faith is intellectual assent to a proposition, such as "God is triune," or "Jesus is divine." The faithful man has the correct beliefs about doctrine, while the unfaithful man is a heretic, or doubter. But this is a bad definition. Faith would have to do with only part of a man's nature—his intellect—while leaving the whole person untouched. Nor does this definition explain why often so-called "heretics" who deny God with "the top of their heads" seem more concerned, more awake, yes, even more Christian than some of the orthodox who affirm God with the "top of the head," but deny him "with the bottom of the heart." [1]

Another definition of faith is centered on man's emotions. Faith is seen as a mystical experience of God, a "feeling" that God is near and real. Surely, every man has awesome experiences when he feels the push of some inexplicable force. Still, this definition deals with only a half man, and stresses individual experience at the expense of the theological tradition of the Christian Church. The mystic is too alone, cut off from the church and often a divisive influence.

A school boy gave a third definition: "Faith is believing something you know isn't true." The worshiper of reason writes faith off as a poor excuse for accepting what his reason rejects. Reason, logic, proof, are the only ways of talking about life. Faith is only wish-dreaming. This definition fails to take into account that reason, logic, and proof are themselves reducible to certain faith assumptions. The worshiper of reason is forced to believe in the orderly process of his own mind in order to reason, and to accept as valid certain proofs while rejecting other proofs *on the basis of faith.*

Faith is not intellectual assent, mystical experience, or wish-dreaming. Faith is trust. This is the way Jesus, Paul, and Augustine used the word. The definition involves the whole man in his total relationship to life, body and soul, mind and emotion.

Trust is necessary to life. There is not a man living who does not place his trust in someone or something, however inadequate the object of his trust may be. As a husband, I trust my wife to behave in a certain way. I invest my life in her and believe that she will keep my confidence. In a similar manner, children trust their parents for clothes, shelter, security, and love. The failure of wife or parent to be trustworthy results in personal crisis. We trust the doctor to know medicine, the electrician to wire our homes, the garbage man to carry away our trash, the cook to keep our food free from poison, and the pilot to fly us safely to our destination. We also trust certain political philosophies, so that one man describes himself as a liberal Democrat, while another as a conservative Republican. Both are making statements about where they put their trust. And "things" play their part in our trust, for things help to make life meaningful. The teenager who told me, "Everything good in life is round—silver dollars, drums, and wheels," gave a brief affirmation of his faith.

Sooner or later, however, the finite objects of trust fail. We find that they are not suitable for our ultimate, or final, trust, for they are doomed to die. We know that life is passing, and we are passing with it. Like shipwrecked sailors, men seek for the permanent among the impermanent, for life in the midst of death. What is not fleeting, fallible, doomed to die? Where can we put our ultimate trust? What will not fail us when everything that we hold valuable is dust?

From the foundations of existence comes an answer. The answer is "God." He, and he alone, is our safe harbor. Faith is not a matter of believing an idea about God, hunting for emotional experiences, or wish-dreaming, but "betting our lives" on God. The question of faith—when it is real—can never be raised as an abstract problem. It always has to do with the whole man involved in all of life.

When we speak of the Christian faith, we speak of a particular way of life. We affirm that we put our ultimate trust in that God who has revealed himself in Jesus Christ and kneel down in obedience to his will. Faith is crying out with Job, "Though he slay me, yet will I trust him" (Job: 13:15, KJV). We serve notice that when we are tempted to worship other gods—to make our object of ultimate trust family, political party, nation, or work—we reject these gods as false and cry out with men of old, "The Lord, he is God; the Lord, he is God" (I Kings 18:39*b*).

The glad invitation is "Come." But we must come with faith, with absolute trust in God. And the paradox is this: What is commanded is given us. Faith is not a relationship to be achieved by our good works, but a gift to be received. We are invited to the Lord's table to receive new faith. This is a sacrament intended to awaken faith in us as surely as the preaching of the Word. All that we need, God supplies. It is God himself who makes us truly human, really free, and faithful to him. So, the man of faith takes no credit for his faith, but can only say with Paul, "Not I, but the grace of God" (I Cor. 15:10*b*).

We have two choices: either we can settle down with a conventional faith, or we can be open to a vital, living trust in God which he is constantly offering. A hundred years ago Søren Kierkegaard wrote a parable about the weak faith of his fellow church members in Denmark. It presented a challenge for an unconventional trust, and is relevant for church members in America. Here is the parable:

Suppose it was so that the geese could talk—then they had so arranged it that they also could have their religious worship, their divine service.

Every Sunday they came together, and one of the ganders preached. The essential content of the sermon was: what a lofty destiny the geese had, what a high goal the Creator (and every time this word was mentioned the geese curtsied and the ganders bowed their head) had set before the geese; by the aid of wings they could fly away to distant regions, blessed climes, where properly they were at home, for here they were only strangers.

So it was every Sunday. And as soon as the assembly broke up each waddled home to his own affairs. And then the next Sunday again to divine worship and then again home—and that was the end of it; they throve and were well-liking, became plump and delicate—and then were eaten on Martinmas Eve—and that was the end of it.

That was the end of it. For though the discourse sounded so lofty on Sunday, the geese on Monday were ready to recount to one another what befell a goose that had wanted to make serious use of the wings the Creator had given him, designed for the high goal that was proposed to him —what befell him, and what a terrible death he encountered.

(Also) among the geese there were some individuals which seemed suffering and grew thin. About them it was currently said among the geese: There you see what it leads to when flying is taken seriously. For because their hearts are occupied with the thought of wanting to fly, therefore they become thin, do not thrive, do not have the grace of God as we have who therefore become plump and delicate.

And then when someone reads this he says: It is very pretty—and that's the end of it. Then he waddles home to his affairs, becomes (or at least endeavors with all his might to become) plump, delicate, fat—but on Sunday morning the parson preachifies . . . and he listens . . . always like the geese.[2]

Come, for all is now ready. Come with faith.

ONE LOAF

John 6:1-14 I Cor. 10:17

After the Duke of Wellington had retired from military service, he attended the parish church to which he belonged. The Lord's Supper was being observed. Following the custom in his church, those wanting to take the sacrament came out of the pews and walked to the Communion rail. When the "Iron Duke" came into the aisle, he was recognized by a former soldier—one who had been the general's personal servant. Elated to see his old commander, the man wanted the others to do him honor. So, he called out, "Make way for His Grace, the Duke of Wellington." Greatly embarrassed, the Duke replied, "No! No! We are all alike here!"

The Duke spoke the truth. "Grace," said P. T. Forsyth, "is the great leveller." Every man is equally loved by God; he plays no favorites. Paul, writing to the Corinthian church, discussed the meaning of the

Lord's Supper. He said, "The cup of blessing which we bless, is it not a participation in the blood of Christ? The bread which we break, is it not a participation in the body of Christ? Because there is one loaf, we who are many are one body, for we all partake of the same loaf." The early Christians observed Communion with only one loaf, from which they tore pieces of bread to eat "in remembrance of him." But Paul referred to more than the bread used in the service: he was speaking about whom the bread symbolized, Jesus Christ.

The bread used in the Lord's Supper has no magical power; it, in itself, does not make us one body. Our participation in the reality that is Christ, our baptism into his community, our recognition of our common Commander makes us one. The Duke of Wellington knew the real Commander when he exclaimed, "No! No! We are all alike here!"

In the Gospel of John, we find the story of the feeding of the five thousand. It is a magnificent story, but unfortunately we often miss the point. We usually record this as a miracle of Jesus, believing that Jesus took a few fishes and bread and fed five thousand hungry people. "So! Wonderful!" we exclaim, and leave it at that. But John's Gospel is disturbingly contemporary. John goes on to record Jesus as saying, "I am the bread of life; he who comes to me shall not hunger, and he who believes in me shall never thirst." In the light of this affirmation, the historic feeding of the five thousand fades into the background. For Jesus as the Christ feeds more than five thousand in ancient Galilee—he feeds you and me. The miracle story was the sign of a far greater reality: Jesus as the true bread now! Jesus as the loaf of life now! Jesus as the One in whom the many may become one now!

Consider, first of all, how this essential unity is true with people. We are many people, aren't we? Go to any large city at rush hour and you will find out how many people we are! Humanity streams out of buildings, piles into automobiles and heads for the freeways—the concrete arteries of the city. More than once I have been caught in the rush hour traffic of Dallas. Always I have regretted it and sympathized with people who must contend with the crowded concrete instead of enjoying the wide open places of North Texas! The rush hour also shows man's striving to get ahead of everyone else without much regard for how we do it—as long as our fenders aren't scratched. Remember T. S. Eliot's words:

> And no man knows or cares who is his neighbour
> Unless his neighbour makes too much disturbance,
> But all dash to and fro in motor cars,
> Familiar with the roads and settled nowhere.[1]

Yes, we are many people—many in number. We are also many in terms of individual characteristics. This is the day of the "Organization Man," where we are often fit into a common mold. The admen try to make us want the same products and do the same things, yet there is a rebellious individuality in us. We may be organization men, but we respond to the organization in a distinctly individual way. There is not one of us who is exactly alike—either in racial stock, ambition, emotion, intellectual qualities, opinions, or what have you. This is the excitement of meeting people: no two are the same.

Yet Paul distinctly says, "We who are many are one body." And when he spoke, he addressed a people who were as different as we in the melting pot of America. For Corinth was the ancient world's melting pot where Jews, Greeks, Romans, and barbarians came together. We are all different, but, in a very real sense, we are all the same! says Paul. He does not try to smooth over differences, but he indicates that in the light of God's grace revealed in Jesus Christ for all men these differences are no longer of real importance.

In John Steinbeck's play-novelette, *Burning Bright,* the unity of mankind is expressed in a story of a middle-aged circus performer Joe Saul and his beautiful wife Mordeen. Joe Saul wanted more than life itself for her to have a baby. His personal immortality was dependent upon reproducing his seed. He had no baby by his first wife, and now it appeared that Mordeen would be barren, too. Deep within him rose the fear that he was sterile. Mordeen feared it, too, and she saw what this was doing to her husband. She made a decision—out of love for him—to make sure that there would be a baby. Imagine Joe Saul's delight when Mordeen announced to him that she was pregnant, but imagine his torment when he discovered that it was another man's son!

Finally, after terrible struggle, he saw that his wife truly loved him and that she wanted by her act to assure him a son. He learned even more. In the hospital, Joe Saul spoke softly to Mordeen:

"I know that what seemed the whole tight pattern is not important. Mordeen, I thought, I felt, I knew that my particular seed had importance over other seed. I thought that was what I had to give. It is not so. I know it now. . . . I had to walk into the black to know—to know that every man is father to all children and every child must have all men as father. This is not a little piece of private property, registered and fenced and separated. Mordeen! This is *the Child*." [2]

Every child is the Child. Everyone has the same Father. Every person is sacred, made in God's image and likeness, and when we are divided from our neighbors, we are divided from God and even from ourselves, since our very life depends upon community together.

Consider, too, how this essential unity is true with the church. It is a sad fact that we do not see unity displayed in most instances. Even at great ecumenical conferences where denominations meet to witness to the Lordship of Christ, the fellowship breaks down at the Lord's Table because of different beliefs about the supper. Thus, the great symbol of Christian unity—the Lord's Supper—becomes an occasion for disunity.

Robert McAfee Brown has suggested a more honest version of "Onward, Christian Soldiers:"

> We are all divided,
> Not one body we,
> One lacks faith, another hope,
> And all lack charity.[3]

Local churches appear like stores competing with one another for customers, seeing who can cut prices the most. We are often smug and satisfied behind our denominational walls, taking pride in statistical gains. Moreover, there is a tendency of every denomination to think that it is the exclusive repository of God's truth. As one preacher who was arguing with another said, "Very well, you may worship God in your way, and I'll worship him in his."

Still, this does not change the truth that the church is Christ's church. He is the Lord and Master over us all; we all find our unity in a common confession of his Lordship. The church is the branch; Christ is the true vine. "Christ is the head of the church . . . Christ loved the church and gave himself up for her." (Eph. 5:23, 25). It is time for judgment to begin at the house of God. We must address words of reconciliation and reunion to ourselves as well as to the world. Denominational pride and division are wounds in the body of Christ.

George Whitefield once preached from the balcony of the old courthouse in Philadelphia. Lifting his eyes as though he could see someone, he dramatically repeated a conversation supposedly taking place above.

"Father Abraham," he cried out, "Who have you in heaven? Any Episcopalians?"
"No!"
"Seeders or Independents?"
"No, No!"
"Why, who do you have there?"
"We don't know those names here. All who are here are Christians, believers in Christ—men who have overcome by the blood of the Lamb and the word of his testimony."
"Oh, is that the case? Then, God help me, God help us all, to forget party names and to become Christians in deed and in truth!"

There is one loaf—Jesus Christ—and because of him, we who are many are one body, for we all partake of the same loaf. To our broken humanity, the gospel word is: You are one in Christ! To our broken church, the good news is: You are one in Christ! And this unity is enacted in the sacrament of the Lord's Supper.

The King of heaven his table spreads,
And blessings crown the board;
Not paradise, with all its joys,
Could such delight afford.[4]

TRUE AND EARNEST REPENTANCE

Matt. 4:17

Chaplain J. Claude Evans of Southern Methodist University wrote, "We do not care for Holy Communion because it makes strange demands upon us, implies that we are sinners in need of forgiveness, a church in need of penitence. And, if this is true or even near the truth, then Holy Communion will not become meaningful for us, until we repent." [1]

The chaplain is a hundred percent right! Taken seriously, Holy Communion shakes the foundations of our lives and turns us upside down, inside out. It is small wonder that people often complain about the service, and stay away when the Eucharist is observed. They invent various excuses, which we have all heard: "I don't like to read all those prayers." "It takes too long." "I don't like to walk down the aisle with other people looking on." But if all hearts were open, all desires known, and no secrets were hid, wouldn't it be obvious that we don't want to be reminded of our need to repent? Even when we come to the service, we attempt to escape the demand to repent. We resist admitting that "we are not worthy so much as to gather up the crumbs under Thy table." We dislike thinking that our lives are in such a fix that we can't do anything about them without the divine invasion of Jesus Christ.

Not wanting to repent, we try to pretend that there is nothing to repent of. We kid ourselves that all's right in our lives, dousing ourselves with the sweet-smelling perfume of secularism as we try to eliminate the stench of our own souls. Modern man is in retreat from himself. Looking at the way Americans spend their weekends is instructive. Instead of relaxing, most Americans engage in a rash of activities designed to have "fun." Throw a party! Get drunk! Go to the lake! Take in a movie! Play golf! Activities pile on top of activities, but we don't find the peace we want. Edward Joseph Shoben, Jr., director of clinical training at Columbia University, tells why: "When fun becomes an instrument of self-deception, it stops being fun." Being on the go-go-go helps us to keep the truth from ourselves, but it costs us the integrity of personality.

Our illusion-making doesn't work for long. Inevitably, we must face ourselves and come to terms with who we really are. Our rationalizations, our elaborate escape mechanisms, will fail us. Indeed, they are already failing. Often when we've never had it so good, the feeling gnaws at our insides that we've never had it so bad. Søren Kierkegaard expressed this paradox when he wrote in his *Journal:* "I have just returned from a party of which I was the life and soul; wit poured from my lips, everyone laughed and admired me—but I went away—and the dash should be as long as the earth's orbit——————————and wanted to shoot myself." A more contemporary example is Marilyn Monroe, the dazzling blond pinup of the Korean G.I. Her name and body flashed on movie screens across the nation. A child of the slums, she climbed the long road to success. She possessed fame, fortune, beauty, talent. Some think that if they had these gifts, life would be worth living. Lest we forget, Marilyn Monroe committed suicide.

The failure of our illusions suggests a second fact about life. Our shattered defenses force us to admit that we are guilty men. One of Marilyn Monroe's husbands, Arthur Miller, wrote a play entitled *All My Sons.* It is about a self-assured businessman named Joe Keller who substitutes faulty material in aircraft. The result is the death of twenty-one pilots. His son Chris is incensed, but Keller justifies himself by saying: "Chris, I did it for you, it was a chance and I took it for you." And: "Chris, a man can't be a Jesus in this world!" The climax of Keller's guilt comes when Chris hands him a letter written by his brother, Larry, who was killed in the war. In it, Larry confesses that he feels guilty for his father.

Yesterday they flew in a load of papers from the States and I read about Dad . . . being convicted. I can't express myself. . . . I can't bear to live any more. Last night I circled the base for twenty minutes before I could bring myself in. How could he have done that? Every day three or four men never return and he sits back there "doing business." . . . I can't face anybody . . . I don't know how to tell you how I feel. . . . I'm going out on a mission in a few minutes. They'll probably report me missing.[2]

The letter crushes Keller's defenses. Suddenly, he realizes that he was responsible for his son Larry's death. And not only his—but those twenty-one men who died because of faulty aircraft material. He sees the truth: *they were all his sons!* Racing upstairs, he kills himself with a single shot.

Keller illustrates the tragedy of a half-repentance which is aware of guilt but not grace. When our defenses are down, when our illusions crumble, when we experience the crisis of guilt, there are only three real alternatives: psychosis, suicide, or repentance.

"Repent, for the kingdom of heaven is at hand!" preached John the Baptist and Jesus Christ. The Greek word for repentance is *metanoia,* which means a change of the whole personality, and the subsequent reordering of one's values. Repentance, when it is genuine, always involves the whole person at a depth level.

We are invited to the Lord's Table in this way: "Ye that do truly and earnestly repent of your sins." Notice the modifiers—true and earnest. Repentance can be a sham and a show, a surface affair and nothing more. But Jesus Christ demands repentance that is true and earnest. We must mean it! We can't be like Augustine and pray, "O Lord, make me pure—but not yet." Our prayer is another one: "Now, O Lord, now is the acceptable time."

Choice is basic to life. Which way will you turn? What kind of person will you become? Answering these questions is unavoidable. Man's freedom does not mean that he is free not to choose. To live is to choose. And choices make the difference. Don't let anybody fool you into thinking otherwise. Remember Robert Frost's poem about "The Road Not Taken."

> Two roads diverged in a yellow wood
> And sorry I could not travel both
> And be one traveler, long I stood
> And looked down one as far as I could
> To where it bent in the undergrowth;
> Then took the other. . . .
>
> I shall be telling this with a sigh
> Somewhere ages and ages hence:
> Two roads diverged in a wood, and I—
> I took the one less traveled by,
> And that has made all the difference.[3]

This, of course, is a parable about life. We go to this school and not another. We choose to be a doctor instead of a lawyer. We marry Sally instead of Sue. We are formed by the choices we make, and we become who we are. And of all the choices that life thrusts upon us, none is more pressing than the question of our ultimate loyalty. Whom shall we worship? God or ourselves? Repentance is not merely turning away from our sins (our self-centeredness); it is turning toward the God who reveals himself in Jesus Christ.

What happens when we repent? Nothing and everything. Nothing in that we are in one sense the same person, with the same memory and the same physical characteristics faced with the same problems and dogged by the same temptations. Everything, for in a more fundamental sense we are each a different person, able to look at life from a new perspective, able to confess our sin instead of trying to hide its reality, able to be ourselves and stop the futile game of pretending. When the French author Sidonie Gabrielle Colette died, her last word was, "*Regarde*." To her, this word suggested look, feel, wonder, accept, live. So with repentance. When we repent, we look, feel, wonder, accept, and live.

"Holy Communion will not become meaningful for us, until we repent," said Chaplain Evans. It is also true that unless we repent, life will not be meaningful for us and, although the kingdom of heaven is at hand, we will not know it.

Fullness of life and Holy Communion are not for the perfect, but they are for the repentant. The invitation to both begins, "Ye that do truly and earnestly repent of your sins."

PRAYER OF OBLATION

Although we say the prayer of oblation every Communion service, the word "oblation" is probably strange and unfamiliar to you. Socrates said, "The unexamined life is not worth living." It is also true that the unexamined ritual is not worth saying. Too long we have repeated words that lacked real meaning for us, and consequently, praying the great traditional prayers degenerates into "heaping up empty phrases."

Oblation means offering. The prayer of oblation is found in the post-communion, after the congregation receives the elements of bread and wine. Yet the mood of oblation runs like a silver thread through the service of Holy Communion, indeed, through every worship service. This prayer reminds us of the basic meaning of corporate worship: the receiving and giving of an offering.

Christians receive an offering before they give one.

It is impossible to worship—especially when we take the Lord's Supper—without remembering that we have received a rich and undeserved inheritance from God. Augustine said, "He loves us as if there were but one of us to love." The nature of God is seeking love, a love which finds man at the deepest level of his being and calls him to live fully and freely. Before man ever reaches to God, God has stretched out his hand. God is not far away, but close. He does not have to be sought; he is the One who seeks.

The foundation of worship is God's offering his Self to us. Notice he offers his Self. God does not offer us a system of ideas, a package of beliefs, or a book of rules. These are sterile and impersonal. God offers his Self in a dynamic personal encounter that enables man to abandon death and darkness and to walk in life and light. At no other place is this Self-offering seen more clearly than in the cross of Jesus Christ. The New Testament writers affirm that the cross is God's purposeful working out of his love. In the death of Jesus Christ, God made the costliest offering of all: the giving of his only Son for our redemption. "God shows his love for us in that while we were yet sinners Christ died for us." "For God so loved the world that he gave his only Son, that whoever believes in him should not perish but have eternal life." The cross means that the God of Abraham, Isaac, and Jacob is also the God of Jones, Smith, and Harris. This God is our Father, and he shows his love for us not for just a moment in time, but for eternity. Every worship service announces that the God who visited other men "at diverse times and sundry places" visits us. We are the sinful community for which Christ died; we are the people whom God loves. God offers his Self in the waters of baptism, in the bread and wine at Communion, in the singing of hymns, the reading of the Scripture; yes, in every act of worship. And not merely here. God offers his Self in every event of life—in the dangers of the world as well as the safety of sanctuary.

What is the Christian community's response to the Self giving of God? When Isaac Watts "surveyed the wondrous cross on which the Prince of Glory died," he was deeply moved. The last verse of his beautiful hymn expresses what we should do:

> Were the whole realm of nature mine,
>   That were an offering far too small;
> Love so amazing, so divine,
>   Demands my soul, my life, my all.[1]

The giving of ourselves in response to God's Self-giving is also at the heart of the prayer of oblation: "And here we offer and present unto thee, O Lord, our selves, our souls and bodies, to be a reasonable, holy, and lively sacrifice unto thee."

Offering has been closely associated with the Eucharist from the first century. The participants were called offerers, instead of communicants. Tertullian said that the Eucharist is a sacrifice, and he regarded the material of the sacrifice as the gifts brought by the people. What were these gifts? The laymen brought bread and wine with them to the Eucharist as part of their responsibility for worship; in turn, the deacons presented the lay offering on the altar. These elements of the field were then consecrated by the priest and distributed to the laymen, only now they had assumed a new meaning. In the Western church, the offering of money at the Eucharist replaced the offering of bread and wine; however, in the Eastern church, the presentation of the elements is still one of the chief acts of the service.

But the offering of things—bread, wine, money—is not a substitute for offering yourself. Offering things symbolizes the offering of yourself to God. Material gifts on the altar should be extension of our personalities. "There you are upon the table," said Augustine to his new communicants when they made their offering of bread and wine. "There you are in the chalice." Of course, we can give things and hold back ourselves. And when this happens, no matter how precious our gift may be, it is an unacceptable sham. God wants only ourselves; we cannot faithfully offer anything in place of the self. The self is the most supremely costly gift, and the only one capable of truly representing our affirmation of God's ultimate worth.

Man's attempts to escape giving his self to God are varied and ingenious. Usually, man gives a part of his life to God while withholding a precious treasure for his own control. He gives God his hands, but not his heart. He gives God his devotional life, but not his political life. He worships God on Sunday, but forgets God in his work. The rich young man who came to Jesus seeking what he must do to inherit eternal life is an illustration. Jesus reminded him of the Jewish law: "Do not kill, Do not commit adultery, Do not steal, Do not bear false witness, Do not defraud, Honor your father and mother." The rich young man replied that he had kept the law from his youth. But the piercing eyes of Jesus searched out the inner man. "You lack one thing; go, sell what you have, and give to the poor, and you will have treasure in heaven; and come, follow me." Why did Jesus make such a demand? Was it not because the young man had allowed his wealth to shut out the light of God from his life? He was unable to give his self to God and the coming kingdom because he had already given his self to material wealth.

Ironically, one of the best ways to escape God's demand for self-giving is by doing good works. The devil's trick is to put us to work doing good and then make us aware of it. At no other time is the temptation for pride greater. When a person is busy doing good—rushing here and there for the church or service club—he can conveniently isolate himself from the one thing needful. The "good" people no less than the "bad" people are tempted to deny God's claim on life.

Give your whole self to God—your talents, your dreams, your work, your recreation, your marriage, your children, your problems. God loves you and wants every bit of you. Hold nothing back, for what you keep from God's consecrating touch is like a poisonous venom surging through your veins.

"But I am not worthy to offer my self to God!" you say. And so should you. We all must confess with Isaiah: "I am a man of unclean lips, and I dwell in the midst of a people of unclean lips." Yet in Jesus Christ, our unacceptable gift has been made acceptable. We who were strangers to God have been reconciled. There is a dramatic scene of self-surrender in Georges Bernanos' *Diary of a Country Priest.*[2] The countess cries in agony: "An hour ago my life seemed so perfectly arranged, everything in its proper place. And you've left nothing standing—nothing at all." The priest says: "Give it to God, just as it is!" She replies: "I'll give Him all or nothing. My people are made that way." "Give everything," challenges the priest. "Oh you don't understand!" she says. "You think you've managed to make me docile. The dregs of my pride would still be enough to send you to hell." The priest is unrelenting: "Give your pride with all the rest! Give everything!" That's the meaning of the prayer of oblation—and of the Christian faith.

HOW TO LOVE YOUR NEIGHBOR

People who regard religion as a personal matter between God and themselves will be uncomfortable as Christians. The cross of Jesus Christ inexorably binds together man's relationship to God and man's relationship to man. Jesus Christ died because he was obedient to the will of the Father and he died because he loved man.

When asked for the great commandment, Jesus gave two that must stand together or else fall apart: "You shall love the Lord your God with all your heart, and with all your soul, and with all your mind. This is the great and first commandment. And a second is like it. You shall love your neighbor as yourself. On these two commandments depend all the law and the prophets" (Matt. 22:37-39).

In the Sermon on the Mount, Jesus taught that one must be reconciled with the brother before he could offer an acceptable gift to God (Matt. 5:23-24) and that we must love our enemies and pray for those who persecute us (Matt. 5:43-44).

The writer of First John bluntly echoed the spirit of Jesus' teachings when he wrote: "If any one says, 'I love God,' and hates his brother, he is a liar; for he who does not love his brother whom he has seen, cannot love God whom he has not seen (I John 4:20)."

The invitation to the Lord's supper follows the biblical pattern when it requires communicants to be "in love and charity with your neighbors." The sacrament is a holy act which we do together. Without community, there can be no Lord's Supper. Taking this sacrament means that we try to love our neighbors even as Christ loved us.

Now, we all flinch from loving our neighbors. It's such a difficult task remembering their names, much less *loving* them! If only our neighbors were different, it might be worth some of the effort to love them. If they were extensions of our own personalities, "things" to be controlled instead of people with independent spirits, we think that life would run much smoother. But as things are, neighbors are always butting into our affairs, infringing on our "rights," disturbing us when we've settled down for an afternoon nap, placing an inconvenient claim on us. Ogden Nash described the matter this way:

> The people upstairs all practice ballet.
> Their living room is a bowling alley.

Their bedroom is full of conducted tours.
Their radio is louder than yours.
They celebrate weekends all the week.
When they take a shower, your ceilings leak.
They try to get their parties to mix
By supplying their guests with Pogo sticks,
And when their orgy at last abates,
They go to the bathroom on roller skates.
I might love the people upstairs wondrous
If instead of above us, they just lived under us.[1]

But the people live upstairs, not downstairs. It is these neighbors with whom we must deal, and not some others. How can you love your neighbor, this other person, sometimes annoying and threatening, to whom you must relate to exist and yet with whom you have a very difficult time existing?

First, recognize that God loves the neighbor as he loves you. There is an old story about a Christian scholar of the sixteenth century named Muretus, who became sick while on a long journey. Some doctors were called in to treat him. Not knowing who he was, they regarded him as a stupid peasant. Speaking to one another in Latin, they said, "Let's try an experiment on this fellow, for he looks of no importance." Muretus then spoke out, also in Latin, "Call not any man cheap for whom Christ died." In the light of the cross, the neighbor—no matter what his religion, race, or disposition—becomes infinitely precious.

Every man is a recipient of God's undeserved love.

Remember that the next time you consign your neighbor to the outer reaches of hell! God loves both you and him. Forgiving love is a possibility for us only as we recognize the depth of our sin and the depth that God has gone to cure it. We cannot neatly divide the population into two groups, the "good guys" (us) and the "bad guys" (our neighbors). All of us are sinners, equally guilty and equally loved by God.

As Ralph Sockman said,

> Gratitude for God's redeeming love thaws the icicled springs of our minds and opens the streams of refreshing memories which flow out in all directions toward our fellowmen. When we recall what God in Christ has done *for* us, we are lifted out of our bitter thoughts about what others are trying to do *to* us.[2]

"Have you ever tried to pray for someone you hated?" a man asked me once, and in such a way as to suggest its impossibility. I believe the reason scores of people have given up praying is that they hold grudges against their neighbors, and they are ashamed to confess this to God. We need to be more honest when we pray. It is not as if we are telling God something he does not already know, for he "knows all hearts." Prayer can be a wrestling through of our most perplexing problems with the neighbor, if we dare to be honest before him.

Whether or not anything happens to the neighbor when we pray, something happens to *us*. Praying for persecutors follows the example Jesus set on the cross when he prayed for those who crucified him, "Father, forgive them; for they know not what they do." This prayer did not change his enemies' attitude toward him, but it held before him God's great love. So with us. There is no guarantee that prayer will make the enemy love us or refrain from persecution, but there is every hope that prayer will help us keep our hearts clean from corrosive hate. And more often than not, when we pray for our neighbors, honestly holding the relationship before our eyes, we are brought to see our own faults, our own injustices, our own pettiness, and our own subtle persecution which we direct to our neighbor.

The third way to love your neighbor is to look below the surface of his actions. We should not be quick to criticize because we never know all the facts about another's motives. An offensive act may have quite a different meaning to the person performing it. For example, little boys who pester little girls make them mad. However, their intention is usually to gain attention and make friends. This is also true on an adult level, where brashness is a common coverup for a genuine desire to be accepted.

We sometimes hurt our neighbors because we don't care enough about them to find out what is going on below the surface. Such a discovery would temper our feelings, perhaps turning our resentment into pity and our pity into creative love. Leslie Weatherhead recalls the story about a prewar luxury cruise which a young girl enjoyed with her friends. The chef, an imaginative man, would bring the ice-cream puddng in some new form every night. One night it was in the shape of the ship itself; another night, a statue; and so on. But one night it was very ordinary, Weatherhead continues, "and the spoiled girl complained to the captain that the chef was getting slack. She did not know that a radio message had reached the chef that his wife was very ill, and that on the night when the ice cream was so ordinary she died." [3]

Finally, work to create a climate of love between you and your neighbor. Whether or not your neighbor loves you is partly dependent on you. Love is a two-way street, and although goodwill toward your neighbor cannot create love in him, bad feelings will certainly work to destroy it. I either build a barrier between my neighbor and myself with acts of deceit, contempt, hostility, and greed, or I help provide soil where the seeds of love are more likely to grow with acts of honesty, respect, peacefulness, and generosity. It is not hypocrisy to act as though you love the neighbor when in fact you do not and pray desperately every day for God to forgive you. Emotions often follow actions, and not the other way around. To imitate love is one way that love may become actual in your relationship with your neighbor.

We are called to be "agents of reconciliation." This is certainly an active, not a passive, vocation. To break down barriers, we cannot afford the safe luxury of waiting for our neighbors to take the initiative—especially if we are Christians. God has come to us; we must go to others. God in Jesus Christ has shown his love for us; we must show our love to others, a love that is grounded in God's love for us. God has suffered for us; so we must suffer for others. It is in this relationship of giving love that we find our true strength. Eric Fromm has said this better than any other modern writer I know.

> In the very act of giving, I experience my strength, my wealth, my power. This experience of heightened vitality and potency fills me with joy . . . Giving is more joyous than receiving, not because it is a deprivation, but because in the act of giving lies the expression of my aliveness.[4]

As we come to the Lord's table, Jesus Christ commands us to love the neighbor. Our confession is that we fail. Our promise is that we will try. May this service remind you of the love of God so freely given to all men and empower you to reflect that love in your relationship with your neighbor.

THOSE WHO HAVE DONE THIS

Luke 22:19

Henry David Thoreau wrote, "A sentence should read as if its author, had he held a plough instead of a pen, could have drawn a furrow deep and straight to the end." Few succeed in doing this. Most of our sentences are clumsy collections of semantic carelessness, shallow and crooked furrows. How refreshing it is to get hold of a book written by someone who knows how to write! On every page, you can see that he is a craftsman, an artist with language, who carefully chooses each word to be a handmaiden of his ideas. When you read such an author, you feel that his is the way a truth should be expressed and to try to say it differently would be a travesty.

I feel this way about some strong sentences from Dom Gregory Dix. I cannot improve on his words; I do not wish to alter them. Give them your attention as you prepare for the Lord's Supper. Dix is writing about the command of Jesus at the last supper, "Do this in remembrance of me." He says:

Was ever another command so obeyed? For century after century, spreading slowly to every continent and country and among every race on earth, this action has been done, in every conceivable human circumstance, for every conceivable human need from infancy and before it to extreme old age and after it, from the pinnacles of earthly greatness to the refuge of fugitives in the caves and dens of the earth. Men have found no better thing than this to do for kings at their crowning and for criminals going to the scaffold; for armies in triumph or for a bride and bridegroom in a little country church; for the proclamation of a dogma or for a good crop of wheat; for the wisdom of the Parliament of a mighty nation or for a sick old woman afraid to die; for a schoolboy sitting an examination or for Columbus setting out to discover America; for the famine of whole provinces or for the soul of a dead lover; in thankfulness because my father did not die of pneumonia; for a village headman much tempted to return to fetich because the yams had failed; because the Turk was at the gates of Vienna; for the repentance of Margaret; for the settlement of a strike; for a son for a barren woman; for Captain So-and-So, wounded and prisoner of war; while the lions roared in the nearby amphitheatre; on the beach at Dunkirk; while the hiss of scythes in the thick June grass came faintly through the windows of the church; tremulously, by an old monk on the fiftieth anniversary of his vows; furtively, by an exiled bishop who had hewn timber all day in a prison camp near Murmansk; gorgeously, for the canonisation of S. Joan of Arc—one could fill many pages with the reasons why men have done this, and not tell a hundredth part of them. And best of all, week by week and month by month, on a hundred thousand successive Sundays, faithfully, unfailingly, across all the parishes of Christendom, the pastors have done this just to *make* the *plebs sancta Dei*—the holy common people of God.

To those who know a little of Christian history probably the most moving of all reflections it brings is not the thought of the great events and the well-remembered saints, but of those innumerable millions of entirely obscure faithful men and women, every one with his or her own individual hopes and fears and joys and sorrows and loves—and sins and temptations and prayers—once every whit as vivid and alive as mine are now. They have left no slightest trace in this world, not even a name, but have passed to God utterly forgotten by men. Yet each of them once believed and prayed as I believe and pray, and found it hard and grew slack and sinned and repented and fell again. Each of them worshipped at the eucharist, and found their thoughts wandering and tried again, and felt heavy and unresponsive and yet knew—just as really and pathetically as I do these things. . . . The sheer stupendous *quantity* of the love of God which this ever repeated action has drawn from the obscure christian multitudes through the centuries is in itself an overwhelming thought. (All that going with one to the altar every morning!) [1]

As Dom Gregory Dix stresses, when we come to communion we participate in an action that has brought Christians together down through the centuries. Great and small, black and white, rich and poor, young and old have gathered to receive the bread and wine at magnificent city cathedrals, simple country meetinghouses, and even outside camp sites. Their lives were immeasurably enriched by participating in this service. We are not alone as we come today. Centuries of Christian practice and tradition are brought together in this action. Thank God for Christian tradition! Thank God for the "great cloud of witnesses" who join with us in full-throated praise, saying "Holy, holy, holy, Lord God of Hosts, heaven and earth are full of Thy glory. Glory be to Thee, O Lord, most high! Amen."

TWO MEN AT COMMUNION

Two men went up to church for the sacrament. One sat and prayed with himself: "God, I thank thee that I am not like other men! I thank thee that we are on right terms, that we have an 'understanding' with one another. Thou hast prospered my life because I have kept thy law. I give thee thanks now for what makes life full and rich—for my split-level house, my T-Bird, my stocks, bonds, and country club membership. Truly, thou hast prospered my life and given me goodness and mercy. I have worked hard, too, Lord. I have not buried my talents in the ground.

"God, I thank thee that for all my good fortune, I have not forgotten others who are in need. I'm not one of the ungrateful who forget how hard it must be at the bottom. I have donated my money to Overseas Relief, the Community Chest, and the church's missions program. Lord, forgive those who forget the poor, and forgive the poor for not being grateful for the help which the enlightened give them.

"God, I thank thee that I am a man of my word. I have never knowingly or purposely cheated anyone in my whole life. Whenever I tell someone something, they know it's the truth. I don't lie. I hate liars.

"God, I thank thee that I am not a victim of race prejudice. Thou dost know how I love the Negroes, Jews, and Mexicans, and how I want programs to help them live better. Forgive all those who hold prejudice in their hearts, and grant unto minority races the understanding of how lucky they are to be Americans, living in this land of the free and home of the brave. Forgive unwise leaders who would try to push their people on those of us who try to help them. Help them see that we are right in our approach to the racial problem.

"God, I thank thee that I am a member of this church. I have watched it grow from its meeting place in a school to a three thousand-member congregation with a budget of over $250,000.00 a year, and from a staff of one minister to a staff of six. Thank thee for the beauty of this building: for the stained glass—particularly for the window dedicated to my parents—for the rich tones of the organ, for the shiny gold cross, for the steeple stretching to the sky. I am particularly thankful for our program of fun and fellowship, and for the like-minded people who worship here. Christian fellowship is so wonderful, Lord, that we should all be more thankful than we are. Be with the minister of our church and grant him wisdom and insight. Help him to stick to the gospel, and not wander off into controversial subjects. Thou must know that we have enough problems without his adding to them.

"God, I thank thee for my family. I wish I had more time to spend with them, but my business takes me out of town so often. They are such a wonderful family, and don't seem to mind. Thou dost know that I give them everything they want. Forgive the unthoughtful husbands who neglect their families.

"God, I thank thee for this country, made great by people who work hard and believe in the free enterprise system. Protect this country from sinister forces that seek to destroy our system—the communists and socialists, the lazy and greedy. Help me this year to expand my business and to pay less income tax."

But the other man would not even lift up his eyes to heaven but beat his breast, praying:

"God, be merciful to me, a sinner! I have no claim on thy grace. There is nothing in my life that would make thee look on me with favor; my soul is filled with darkness. I have wasted my life. Holding in my hands the symbols of Christ's body and blood, I have remembered Paul's warning that whoever eats and drinks unworthily is eating and drinking damnation to himself. I wondered how many others were unworthy, forgetting that the words were also addressed to *me.* Forgive me, Lord, for being hard on others and easy on myself, for criticizing the speck in my brother's eye while forgetting the log in my own.

"God, be merciful to me a sinner! I have done those things which I ought not to have done, and I have left undone those things which I ought to have done. I am the sick part of a sick thing. There is no health in me. I have wandered far from my father's house, sinning against heaven and before thee, not worthy to bear the name of Christ. I have been guilty of substituting the gift of things for the gift of self. I have found it easier to write checks for benevolent activities than to engage personally in helping the distressed. I have desired success and status more than obedience to thy will.

"God be merciful to me a sinner! I make great promises to thee in prayer, but do not keep them in practice. Surrounded by the safe walls of the church, it is easy to intone thy name. But surrounded by the danger of the world, thy name comes hard. It is so difficult to witness to my faith. In truth, I have given up trying.

"God, be merciful to me a sinner! As I take the sacrament today, may I participate in the new life which thou dost offer. May I shed my old life like a worn-out suit of clothes, and put on the Lord Jesus Christ. I come to Communion, not trusting in my own righteousness, but in thy manifold and great mercies. I acknowledge my guilt before thee, and pray for forgiveness."

"I tell you, this man went down to his house justified

rather than the other; for every one who exalts himself will be humbled, but he who humbles himself will be exalted" (Luke 18:14).

"If we say we have no sins, we deceive ourselves, and the truth is not in us. If we confess our sins, he is faithful and just, and will forgive our sins and cleanse us from all unrighteousness" (I John 1:8-9).

THE SIGNIFICANCE OF SYMBOLS

Man can no more live without symbols than without water and air. We are not disembodied spirits, floating in the air, able to get along on the "spiritual" and "invisible." Our spirits seek expression through our bodies; material forms are by necessity conveyers of spiritual realities. Too often, well-intentioned "spiritualists" have attempted to scuttle the material emphasis of Christianity. The early Gnostics taught that Jesus only "appeared" to be in human form, and their modern counterpart—Christian Science—suggests that the material is only an illusion. But the mainstream of the Christian church always votes squarely for the material: Jesus Christ was truly flesh and blood man, and the material is real, part of God's creation. There is nothing evil about the material in itself. C. S. Lewis put the matter succinctly: "God likes matter; He invented it."

It has always puzzled me that some people are so dead set against symbols in religion, while they make use of symbols in their everyday lives, indeed, find them indispensable. A friend of mine began wearing a robe in a church which was not accustomed to this ministerial way of dressing. A wave of protest swept the congregation, and the fear was voiced that their minister had become a convert to Rome. Yet the robe is a perfectly legitimate Protestant symbol of the ministry! I have known others who look with great suspicion on the traditional Christian symbols, such as the hand, fish, crown, and even the cross. Under the influence of Puritanism, some churches have felt that keeping the building bare of traditional symbols preserved them from the danger of breaking the second commandment. They forget that anything—especially theological ideas—is capable of becoming an idol! Then, too, the resistance against symbols has not left untouched the two sacraments, Baptism and Holy Communion. Many churches hide their baptismal fonts, and use the altar only for candles and the Bible. I know of a large church where the altar is pushed to one side of the pulpit and never used for observing the Eucharist. Instead, the congregation is invited to take the sacrament—if they would like—in a brief chapel service after the "preaching service." Surely such sacramental negligence happens only when congregation and clergy have lost sight of the importance of symbols for a vital faith. New emphasis on the sacramental life of the church will not answer all our problems, but it will go a long way to recall us to the central meaning of the Christian Church: the life, death, and resurrection of Christ and his summons to a new humanity.

I think that it is important to show exactly the prominant role symbols play in our daily lives. Take Mr. Jones, for example. He comes to church, gripes about the minister's robe, the new *Agnus Dei* window and the length of the Communion service. "All folderol!" he grunts to his wife as they drive home. "I wish that the church would get back to the simplicity of Christ." After they arrive home, Mr. Jones rummages around the garage and finds the Stars and Stripes. He goes to the front of the house, and attaches the flag to a holder. It is the Labor Day Weekend, and Mr. Jones believes that he should fly the flag on national holidays. A few minutes pass; a car door slams in the driveway. The Joneses' son and his family have arrived for lunch. Mr. Jones runs to the door, opens it, and greets everyone with a resounding "hello." He shakes hands with his son, kisses his daughter-in-law on the cheek, and embraces the grandchildren. Mrs. Jones joins in the greeting. Later at the dinner table, the family holds hands as Mr. Jones says the blessing. In the middle of the afternoon, the grandchildren persuade grandfather to play soldier with them. Naturally, he is selected as the general. The children salute him, and quickly the smiling Mr. Jones touches his forehead with his right hand as he returns the salute.

Mr. Jones—the same Mr. Jones who thought symbols were inappropriate in church and desired simplicity—employs no less than half a dozen symbols in one afternoon to express himself. He hung the *flag, shook hands* with his son, *kissed* his daughter-in-law, *hugged* his grandchildren, *joined* hands for the blessing, and *saluted* his grandchildren. For Mr. Jones to have attempted to spend that Sunday afternoon without employing such symbols would have been next to impossible. And failure to use the symbols of affection with his son's family would have seemed incredible to them, suggesting serious estrangement.

As Mr. Jones could not live one Sunday afternoon without the use of symbols, Mr. Jones's church cannot live without symbols. Symbols are necessary for the valid proclamation of the gospel. The sacraments are symbols which have been elevated to a special place in the life and worship of the church. In obedience to Christ's command, the sacraments should be celebrated regularly to remind the church of what God has done in Jesus Christ. A sacrament, goes a well-known definition, is "an outward and visible sign of an inward and spiritual grace." In other words, a sacrament is a spiritual reality taking on material form in order that the reality might be more readily appropriated by the community of faith.

God comes to man at every corner of his being. He leaves nothing free from his consecrating touch. God appeals to us through the audible word, but he is also present in the sacraments. Significantly, the Reformers referred to the sacraments as "visible words." There is no strict division between Word and Sacrament; both are parts of an indivisible whole. The sacraments are God's way of reaching us through sight and touch and taste—making an appeal to us through senses other than hearing. And how we need this! Goethe went to the heart of the matter when he said that the highest cannot be spoken; it can only be acted.

But what does God purpose to do in the sacraments? The same thing he sought to do in Jesus Christ and the same thing he seeks to do in the Holy Spirit and in the preaching of the Word. God desires that man be reconciled to him. In every event of life, God is the seeking father earnestly wanting us prodigals to return home. The sacraments are God's kiss, his embrace, his handshake, indicating that he has nothing but love toward us and desires that our estrangement be overcome. Baptism is God's "sacrament of prevenient grace" in which he proclaims that he is seeking man before man seeks him. The Eucharist is the "sacrament of suffering love," in which God demonstrates his love so freely given in Jesus Christ.[1] But this is not an empty demonstration, which refers to something that happened in the past tense. The sacraments are more than bare tokens or signs; they are ways by which the Holy Spirit actually affects us, moves in our hearts and awakes our faith. As J. S. Whale said, "The Sacraments do not add anything to the Word, any more than the kiss and the ring add anything to plighted troth. But they do movingly reiterate it; they give effect to it." [2] This is why the sacraments are often called "means of grace." This phrase suggests that sacraments are major ways through which God reaches his church with his forgiving love.

God is at work in our lives to bring us back to himself. He does not force us to love him, but like an understanding parent, he wins our trust and confidence. In order that we might be reconciled to him, he uses symbols, ritual, liturgy, concrete and material means which we call sacraments. Baron von Hügel wrote: "I kiss my child not only because I love it; I kiss it also in order to love it." The Christian might say that we participate in Holy Communion not only because we love God, but also *in order* to love him. The action helps to sustain our faith in him.[3]

"I wish that the church would get back to the simplicity of Christ," was Mr. Jones's plea. Well, the church is never simpler than when the sacraments are celebrated. Truly, Christ instituted them for the simple—for us frail human beings—who need to see and touch and taste, as well as to hear, the Word.

CHRIST IN DISGUISE

Matt. 25:34-40

J. D. Salinger's *Franny and Zooey*[1] is an engaging novel about two completely different people who happen to be brother and sister.

Franny is a mystic, who tries to achieve oneness with God by repeating a Buddhist-like "Jesus prayer" over and over until it becomes a very part of her heartbeat. It goes: "Lord Jesus Christ, have mercy on me." She got the idea from a book, which belonged to her deceased brother, Seymour. Zooey is a practical, down-to-earth fellow, whose I.Q. allows him to be anything he wants. He chose to be a television actor, and has achieved considerable success. The family from which they come—the Glass family—is an unusual one. The mother and father were vaudeville entertainers. All their children—five boys and two girls—were recognized geniuses, even though an age span of eighteen years separates the eldest from the youngest. For sixteen years, they thrilled radio audiences on a children's quiz show, "It's a Wise Child." The book hinges on Franny's behavior, and on Zooey's confronting her with herself.

In the last pages of the book, Zooey recalls an incident with his brother Seymour. Zooey was substituting for his brother Walt on "It's a Wise Child," and Seymour had told him to shine his shoes. This made Zooey furious. He thought that the studio audience, the announcer, the sponsor were all morons. Zooey wasn't about to shine his shoes for them, he told Seymour. But Seymour told him to do it for the Fat Lady, Zooey told Franny. And every time he ever went on the air again, he shined his shoes for Seymour's Fat Lady.

Zooey says that he pictured the Fat Lady sitting on a porch all day, swatting flies, with her radio going full blast. And she probably had cancer. Franny became very excited when Zooey told her this. Once Seymour had told her to be funny for the Fat Lady. And Franny had visualized her much the same as Zooey: "I didn't ever picture her on a porch, but with very—you know —very thick legs, very veiny. I had her in an awful wicker chair. She had cancer, *too,* though, and she had the radio going full-blast all day! Mine did, too!"

Then, Zooey tells who the Fat Lady is:

> I don't care where an actor acts. It can be in summer stock, it can be over a radio, it can be over television, it can be in a . . . Broadway theatre, complete with the most fashionable, most well-fed, most sunburned-looking audi-

ence you can imagine. But I'll tell you a terrible secret . . . *There isn't anyone out there who isn't Seymour's Fat Lady* . . . There isn't anyone *any*where that isn't Seymour's Fat Lady. Don't you know that? Don't you know that . . . secret yet? And don't you know—*listen* to me, now—don't you know who that Fat Lady really is? . . . Ah, buddy. Ah, buddy. It's Christ Himself. Christ Himself, buddy.

For Franny, the turning point in her life was this conversation with Zooey. The Fat Lady of Seymour's was, at first, a mythical character who appeared in the minds of Franny and Zooey. But Zooey came to recognize that the Fat Lady was concrete in every person everywhere—"There isn't anyone *any*where that isn't Seymour's Fat Lady." And the Fat Lady is a symbol for Christ.

Where is Christ to be found? The answer is, of course, everywhere. God does not limit the revelation of himself, but meets us in all corners of existence. Even that which is against God—our sin—can be made to point us to him. Still, he is more likely to meet us in some places than in others. He is more likely to meet us in the service of Holy Communion than at a cocktail party; we can find him in a person easier than in a stone or a tree. In the twenty-fifth chapter of Matthew, Christ is recorded as saying he is most likely to come in the crying needs of persons, unlovely and unromantic though these are. To those on his right hand, the Lord said:

Come, O blessed of my Father, inherit the kingdom prepared for you from the foundation of the world; for I was hungry and you gave me food, I was thirsty and you gave me drink, I was a stranger and you welcomed me, I was naked and you clothed me, I was sick and you visited me, I was in prison and you came to me." Then the righteous will answer him, "Lord, when did we see thee hungry and feed thee, or thirsty and give thee drink? And when did we see thee a stranger and welcome thee, or naked and clothe thee? And when did we see thee sick or in prison and visit thee?" And the King will answer them. "Truly, I say to you, as you did it to one of the least of these my brethren, you did it to me" (Matt. 25:34-40).

These words stab us awake. They do not allow us to be complacent when we meet the neighbor, but call us into an awareness that the neighbor whom we confront—whether we call him friend or enemy—is Christ in disguise. Popular piety has made the mistake of painting a stereotyped picture of the historical Jesus as an attractive man—tall, with straight nose, friendly eyes, and radiant face—a person you would want to include on the invitation list to a party. But the twenty-fifth chapter of Matthew suggests that Seymour's picture of Christ as the Fat Lady may be closer to reality than Sallman's Head of Christ! The word here is that Christ is incarnate in the unattractive, even the repulsive, neighbor whose empty hands plead for help.

Look at the "least of these my brethren" with whom Jesus identified himself: the hungry and thirsty, who eat scraps like dogs and still die of malnutrition; the strangers, who have no friends; the naked, who lack adequate clothing or housing to keep them warm and who die of exposure; the sick, who despair in their pain and loneliness; the prisoners, who are rejected by society for crimes that society helped produce. If Christ is no longer a reality to us—if we have "lost" him—then it is because we have tried to. We have lost him because we refuse to look over the neatly trimmed hedges of our suburban plenty into the troubled world outside where people lack material necessities.

But we should not think of need merely on the level of the material, important as this is. There is another level that touches us all: the spiritual. Everyman hungers and thirsts for the bread and water of life; everyman is naked inside, longing for protective clothing; everyman is a stranger, ignorant of who he is, longing to be a whole person; everyman is sick at heart, crying to be well; everyman is caught in the prison of time, beating on the bars to win freedom. In our gadget-filled suburban paradise, we know the meaning of hell. Despite the melodic flow of the stereo, we have not been able to shut out the persistent question: "What is the meaning of life?" Riding on the wave of unparalleled economic success, we make more, but enjoy it less.

We stand in need, and thus we are unattractive to ourselves as needful men. We dislike admitting that we have needs which cannot be instantly supplied by lifting the telephone receiver and dialing a number. Such an admission forces us to recognize our place before God as creatures, and not as the Creator. Nevertheless, we *are* creatures. We cannot fulfill our own needs as isolated individuals, but must turn to the community for wholeness. And ultimately, we must turn to God for the fulfillment of our deepest need: the overcoming of estrangement.

Today, we take the sacrament of the Lord's Supper. It is a meal of sacrificial service, not only reminding us that Christ poured out his blood and allowed his body to be broken for us, but also challenging us to dedicate ourselves to the service of our neighbors in his name. To participate in the Lord's Supper is to unite ourselves to Christ, willing that our blood be spilled and our bodies broken for the sake of the neighbor.

Those whom we serve may not be witty, intelligent, charming, or attractive. They may not be white Anglo-Saxon Protestants. We may feel dogged and depressed by their company. Franny and Zooey did not see the Fat Lady as an attractive person. Her radio was going full blast all day, and she was dying with cancer. Franny saw her with "thick legs, very veiny." The Fat Lady may be cantankerous, self-pitying, selfish. Still she is the neighbor. And: "don't you know who the Fat Lady really is? . . . Ah, buddy. Ah, buddy. It's Christ Himself. Christ Himself, buddy."

The New Testament uses many titles for Jesus: "King," "Savior," "Redeemer," "Son of God," "Lord,"

"Christ." But in our scripture reading, Christ is spoken of as the neighbor who needs the ministry of love. Christ comes to us in disguise as Seymour's Fat Lady, the neighbor. And to find him as Lord, we must also find him as the Fat Lady. When you take Communion, remember the words of Christ when he said: "Truly, I say to you, as you did it to one of the least of these my brethren, you did it to me."

WATER BECOMES WINE

John 2:10

Galilean weddings were times for rejoicing, dancing, laughing, joking, talking, eating, and drinking. A wedding feast was public, not private, taking on the character of a community celebration. Families who were united by the marriage of a son and a daughter wanted to share their happiness with friends and neighbors. The feast lasted seven days, with new guests arriving regularly.

Jesus entered an atmosphere filled to overflowing with happiness. And there is absolutely no hint that he felt discomfort about the levity. Rather, there is every indication that he was at home with the happiness. Unlike John the Baptist, he was no ascetic who wore a hair shirt. He came to make joy full and complete.

During the course of the celebration, the wine supply ran out. Jesus and his disciples were probably unexpected guests and, although the host made careful provisions, they had put too much of a strain on the wine supply. Imagine the embarrassment of the householder when he found that the wine was gone! His feelings were shared by the mother of Jesus, who called her son's attention to the emergency: "They have no wine." Jesus' reply seems unduly harsh: "O woman, what have you to do with me? My hour has not yet come." However, in Hebrew, "woman" is a polite form of address and the phrase following contains no note of harshness in the original Greek. A better translation is: "Never mind. Don't be worried."

Mary apparently caught this meaning, for she commanded the servants to follow his orders. Jesus told them to fill huge jars with water, and to take a sample to the steward of the feast. The servants did so and, behold, the steward tasted wine! Not knowing where the wine came from, the steward called to the bridegroom and said: "Every man serves the good wine first; and when men have drunk freely, then the poor wine; but you have kept the good wine until now."

This story is the cornerstone of John's Gospel. It proclaims how sufficient Christ is in every difficulty, how he enters into our problems, and how he transforms flat lives into an amazing fullness. But, of course, not everyone sees this in the Galilean. Christ's work is hidden, open only to the eyes of faith. The steward of the feast did not know who provided the good wine. The servants knew, but there is no evidence that they recognized the significance. Only to his disciples did

Jesus show his glory. Faith is not a matter of believing in a miracle; faith is a matter of believing and then seeing the miracle. The miracles were "signs" which pointed away from themselves to eternal truths about the kingdom; Jesus did not use miracles as clubs to coerce the naïve into the kingdom of God. The real miracle in the New Testament is always Jesus Christ himself.

Jesus did not transform the water to accommodate the host, but to proclaim a central truth about his message and mission to his disciples. This miracle at Cana of Galilee was a sacramental act—"an outward and visible sign of an inward and spiritual grace." To the early Christian community who worshiped by breaking bread and drinking wine, this incident reminded them of the Lord's Supper. The wine became visible words by which Jesus announced, "Come unto me, you who are beaten down by the winds of life and I will give you courage. You have drunk of flat water, but I make all things new. I accept you as you are, and I make your life tasteful wine. You can have joy such as you have never known before: the joy of my presence. I will never leave you no matter what happens. I come so that you will be able to taste the joy of abundant life."

And we desperately want the joy which Jesus Christ offers us. Throughout history, man has searched for joy with extremes that appall us when we consider the grotesque attempts. We take the good creation and attempt to discover joy by distorting God's purposes so that even the very creation itself seems corrupt. Take sex, for example. It is part of God's creation and, as such, is good. God intended that sex be used to glorify him, to be a reminder of his mercy and a symbol of love between man and wife. The sexual relationship is meant to be responsible, entered into by those who agree before God "to love and to cherish till death do us part." But man has distorted and twisted sex to serve selfish ends so that some consider sex the essence of evil.

Man is taking a roller-coaster ride. The slow pull uphill and our hearts beat faster in anticipation. The top. Plunging down. Round the curve. Start the climb. Over again. Hell. Man tries everything on his wild ride: liquor, sex, entertainment, food, affluence. But none succeed. Disappointed, man continues his ride searching for the joy which is always around the next curve. His search sometimes becomes so distorted that he is able to enjoy himself only by inflicting pain on others. So enters the sadist who glories in the misery of his fellow human beings.

Artificial ways of producing joy have failed us. And small wonder. We cannot enjoy the creation without the Creator. Joy is not ours to summon or to produce. Joy is a gift to be received. Like the prodigal son, we find that it is impossible to find joy outside the father's house. Outside, we starve to death on a pig's diet. But inside the house—could that be the secret? Could it be that we have started at the wrong end? We have searched for joy as a thing in itself, but joy is the by-product of a healthy relationship to the Lord and Giver of Life.

Joy seeks us out of the depths of life. We are no more able to seek joy and find it than a fish can change its home from the ocean to dry land. Joy comes to us and, ironically, does not appear as itself. Joy comes in the form of the despised and rejected Jesus of Nazareth. As his miracles were open only to the eyes of faith, the joy of following him is also hidden—open only to the eyes of faith. Joy is hidden on the cross where the lonely Christ cried out in agony, "My God, my God, why hast thou forsaken me?" The testimony of Christians is that by following this One and identifying ourselves with the suffering and pain of the world, we open our lives for the coming of joy.

There is joy inside the Father's mansion. Jesus Christ is always and forever the honored guest at the marriage feast. But you will never know it unless you come in. Outside, the music is muted and the light is dim. *You must come into the Father's house before you can know music and light and joy.* "I will arise and go to my father!" is a necessary prelude to joy.

The steward of the feast said to the bridegroom, "Every man serves the good wine first; and when men have drunk freely, then the poor wine; but you have kept the good wine until now." This probably referred to a common custom in ancient Galilee. To save money, the host would often save the poor wine for later when the guests' taste was dulled by too much wine. John, the

Evangelist, meant a play on words. The statement referred not only to wine, but also to Jesus Christ. John was saying that God had kept the good wine until now, until the fullness of time when he came in Jesus Christ. God does not shortchange us! He does not run short. Fellowship with him is like climbing a mountain —always we are moving higher. We thought that we knew great joys yesterday in his service, but they were small compared to now, and now will be small compared to tomorrow.

At every moment in life—in this very moment as we draw near to the table—Christians are able to exclaim with thanksgiving: "You have kept the good wine until now."

NOTES

Advent: WAITING FOR GOD

1. Samuel Beckett, *Waiting for Godot,* Act. I. Trans. from his original French text by the author. Copyright © 1954 by Grove Press.
2. "The Trail of the Dinosaur," *Encounter* (London) (May, 1955).
3. *Prisoner for God* (New York: The Macmillan Company, 1954), p. 164.

Christmastide: GOD'S GREAT TRIP

1. *Travels with Charlie* (New York: The Viking Press, 1962), p. 10.
2. Michael Daves, "Incarnation." Reprinted from *motive* (December, 1960), by permission. Copyright © 1960 by the Division of Higher Education of The Methodist Church.

New Year's: GOD AND OUR ANXIETY

1. Roland H. Bainton, *Here I Stand* (Nashville: Abingdon Press, 1959), pp. 28-36.
2. From "September 1, 1939," copyright 1940 by W. H. Auden. Reprinted from *The Collected Poetry of W. H. Auden,* by permission of Random House, Inc., and by permission of Faber & Faber, Ltd., London.

NOTES

Epiphany: THE LIGHT OF THE WORLD

1. Michael Daves, "Wise Men from the University." Reprinted from *motive* (December, 1959), by permission. Copyright © 1960 by the Division of Higher Education of The Methodist Church.
2. Quoted by Alec R. Vidler in *Christian Belief* (New York: Charles Scribner's Sons, 1950), p. 117.
3. Alfred, Lord Tennyson, "In Memoriam."

Lent: THE LORD'S DEATH

1. Isaac Watts, "When I Survey the Wondrous Cross."

Eastertide: NOT A FUNERAL SERVICE!

1. Horatius Bonar, "Here, O My Lord, I See Thee."

Confirmation: "THE WHOLE ARMOR OF GOD"

1. T. George Harris, "Memo About a Dallas Citizen," *Look* (August 11, 1964), p. 64.
2. *The Journals of Kierkegaard,* trans. Alexander Dru (Glasgow: Fontana Books Edition), p. 147.

Pentecost: FOUR ROOMS

1. *The Young Church in Action* (New York: The Macmillan Company, 1955), p. vii.
2. Isaac Watts, "I'll Praise My Maker."

Independence Sunday: UNLEAVENED BREAD

1. Quoted in Leslie F. Church, *Knight of the Burning Heart* (New York and Nashville: Abingdon-Cokesbury Press, n.d.), pp. 168-69.

Labor Sunday: HOLY COMMUNION AND WORK

1. See John A. T. Robinson, *On Being the Church in the World* (Philadelphia: The Westminster Press, 1962), pp. 64-65.
2. Robert Raines, "Conversion Within the Church," Yokefellow House. Italics added.
3. From *Quotable Poems,* Vol. II by Thomas Curtis Clark. ("When Through the Whirl of Wheels" by G. A. Studdert-Kennedy) reprinted by permission of Harper & Row, Publishers, Incorporated. "Then Shall He Come" reprinted by permission of Hodder and Stoughton Limited.

Thanksgiving: "HE . . . GAVE THANKS"

1. *Prisoner for God,* p. 67.
2. Reprinted by permission of Carlotta Monterey O'Neill and Yale University Press from *Long Day's Journey into Night,* by Eugene O'Neill. Copyright 1955 by Carlotta Monterey O'Neill.

COME WITH FAITH

1. See John Baillie, *Our Knowledge of God* (New York: Charles Scribner's Sons, 1959).
2. "The Tame Geese," as told by Cornelius Loew, in *Modern Rivals to Christian Faith* (Philadelphia: The Westminster Press, 1956), pp. 94-95.

ONE LOAF

1. From Chorus II of "The Rock" in *Collected Poems 1909-1962* by T. S. Eliot. Reprinted by permission of Faber and Faber Ltd., London, and Harcourt, Brace and World, Inc.
2. *Burning Bright,* Act 3, Scene 2 (New York: The Viking Press, Inc., 1950), pp. 156, 158.
3. *The Spirit of Protestantism* (New York: Oxford University Press, 1961), p. 24.
4. Philip Doddridge, "The King of Heaven His Table Spreads."

TRUE AND EARNEST REPENTANCE

1. *The Word, the World, and the Sacrament* (Nashville: Board of Education of The Methodist Church, 1963), p. 37.
2. *All My Sons,* Act 3 (New York: The Viking Press, Inc.).
3. From "The Road Not Taken" from *Complete Poems of Robert Frost.* Copyright 1916, 1921 by Holt, Rinehart and Winston, Inc. Copyright 1944 by Robert Frost. Reprinted by permission of Holt, Rinehart and Winston, Inc.

PRAYER OF OBLATION

1. Isaac Watts, "When I Survey the Wondrous Cross."
2. *Diary of a Country Priest* (Glasgow: Fontana Books Edition), p. 148.

HOW TO LOVE YOUR NEIGHBOR

1. "The People Upstairs," by Ogden Nash.

2. "'The Roots of the Reconciling Message," *The Pulpit* (May, 1964), p. 21.
3. *When the Lamp Flickers* (Nashville: Abingdon Press, 1948), p. 162.
4. *The Art of Loving* (New York: Harper & Row, 1956), p. 23.

THOSE WHO HAVE DONE THIS

1. Dom Gregory Dix, *The Shape of the Liturgy* (London: Dacre Press: A & C Black, Ltd., 1945), pp. 744-45.

THE SIGNIFICANCE OF SYMBOLS

1. See Gustaf Aulen, *The Faith of the Christian Church* (rev. ed.; Philadelphia: Fortress Press, 1961).
2. *Christian Doctrine* (New York: The Macmillan Company, 1941), p. 159.
3. See Donald M. Baillie, *The Theology of the Sacraments* (New York: Charles Scribner's Sons, 1957) for the basic idea contained in this paragraph.

CHRIST IN DISGUISE

1. J. D. Salinger, *Franny and Zooey* (Boston: Little, Brown and Co., 1961).